JESUS CRIED

TWO INVISIBLE SUPER POWERS

PRELUDE:

TWO OF THE LONGEST ENEMIES, WE DO NOT SEE THEM BUT THEY SEE US ALL THE TIME!

THEY DO NOT NEED WEAPONS, GUNS, TANKS OR WARSHIPS TO FIGHT, BUT THEY HAVE SPIRIT! THEY TOLD ME I WILL BECOME ONE OF THEM.

FOLLOW ME ON THIS JOURNEY; I'LL TAKE YOU TO THE TRUTH.

I WILL GIVE YOU ALL THE TOOLS TO PUT THE PUZZLES TOGETHER TO FIND THE TRUTH.

SHORT STORY BY:

JAMSHID MORRVARIDY

DEDICATION PAGE

I DEDICATE THIS BOOK TO OUR ONLY CREATOR

ALSO LIKE TO THANK

OTTO

PETER

ERNESTINE

DAVE

WITHOUT YOUR FAITH AND MESSAGES, I WOULD NOT HAVE BEEN ABLE TO COMPLETE MY JOURNEY.

MY GOALS IN WRITING THIS BOOK ARE TO FURTHER HELP SPREAD THE WORD OF OUR FATHER & TO HELP GOD'S FOLLOWERS PREPARE FOR THE RETURN OF JESUS CHRIST.

PLEASE HELP HOWEVER YOU CAN, EITHER BY SPREADING THE LORD'S WORD EVEN BY CHANGING THE MIND OF ONE PERSON TO HELP THEM BE SAVED IS A BLESSING IN ITSELF.

**ALL PROCEEDS WILL BE USED TO HELP THE
HOMELESS AND SICK.**

REFERENCES ARE FROM:

DOVE OF PEACE AUTHORIZED KING JAMES VERSION
COPYRIGHT 1960, 1963, 1965

LIFE APPLICATION BIBLE FROM THE LIVING BIBLE
COPYRIGHT 1971

FOR GOD SO LOVED THIS WORLD, THAT HE GAVE HIS ONLY BEGOTTEN SON,

THAT

WHOEVER

BELIEVETH IN

HIM SHOULD

NOT PERISH,

BUT HAVE

EVERLASTING

LIFE.

JOHN 3:16

Introduction:

I have to tell this story for the world to understand the evils that are present and what is about to happen to many poor souls. This is a short story of my journey. The great signs and miracles that happened along the way, even though I did not understand them all at that time, but when I did finally understand and I put the puzzles together, then it all made sense. This is the salvation of my soul. How I struggled dealing with day-to-day life, but now I know where my place is in this world. What I need to accomplish, and the goals I need to obtain, and with the help of the invisible superpower, how I will reach my goals for myself and all who struggle.

It is a beautiful and terrible thing, and, therefore, should be treated with great caution. Whether you agree with me or not, I wish for the protection of innocent souls so that temptations that he or she may have fallen prey to can be saved because there is a terrible price to pay.

Hi, my name is Jamshid Morrvaridy, born in Iran on 12/07/1966.

I have a story to tell the world, but before I tell you who we are, where we come from, what's going on in this world, and where exactly we go after this world.

I need to tell you about myself, my past, and my present in this first chapter, then in the second part, I explain who Jesus is and about heaven. I explain the earth and the heaven. This is very important that you know where we originally come from and where we are heading. The purpose of this book is to add to your knowledge of who you are, who your only creator is and also to help and feed the homeless and sick people around the world.

I have written this book in the simplest way that I could; there is nothing hard and complex to understand. All the evidence, signs, and miracles are marked and revealed in this book. This story is about actual times and places that I can remember. Where I had been is confirmed by the witnesses. Every point is very important for your knowledge. There is nothing fake or hidden in this book.

My recommendation is you only need to be patient and have complete focus while reading the entire book; if you don't get the points in your first reading, I suggest reading the entire book a couple more times. If you are not interested in knowing the reality and the truth, then this is not for you, and if you don't have the patience to learn the truth about Jesus, then I suggest you please don't waste your time and money.

Again, please be very patience with me throughout the whole book; I am telling you my life story and my journey to the one and only creator.

Map of my journey where I started in 1966 and where I ended up in 2022.

Chapter 1

This is a summary of my past and my present; I will start when I was a kid, about 4 years old, until my present.

When I was 3 or 4 years old living in Iran, my parents divorced. I lived with my dad until I was 10 years old. I was beaten and slapped often. This was also during the war between Iran and Iraq, where many children were recruited as suicide bombers. These are not a good memory. Then I moved in with my mom, but I still wasn't happy and had some more bad memories. I lived with my Mom and sister until I was 17 years old. These were such horrible times; childhood was very difficult and troubling. During this time, though, I learned most of the music theories by myself without any music teacher. I started learning piano first, and then I jumped to guitar.

I left my mother's about the same time; there was something like a negative energy that would bother me every day. I didn't know or understand what it was, but it wanted me to think and stay in the past to hold onto the bad memories; this feeling kept my mind inside an empty box, something that did not want me to think out of the box.

When I left my mother's home, there were times that I had to live and sleep in the parks or somewhere else. I did have a plan; somehow, I had to leave my country of Iran.

One night, perhaps around midnight, when I was laying on the bench inside the dark park, I heard somebody talk to me like he was very close to me, but I saw nobody around me. It was only a voice in the darkness of the park. That voice told me, **"WHERE EVER YOU GO, THE SKY IS THE SAME."** I looked around to see who was talking to me, but I saw no one around me. Please remember this. I have a point and reason for mentioning this. Further explanation is in the conclusion.

In order for me to leave the country, I had to work and make some money. I worked for a distant family member for a year and a half and made some money, but his son, who didn't want to work, told me he could work with my money and make the money double. I trusted him; I gave him the money but did not see him ever again. I found another job somewhere else and made some money.

Then, I thought it was time to leave this country. I got my passport and left the country on a bus. I went to Turkey when I was 20 years old. From Turkey, I met a smuggler who created a fake passport for me and my fake wife; we went to Bulgaria, Yugoslavia and finally got to Ostrich. I became a refugee in that country. I ended up in Hitler's refugee camps from World War II, big, tall, and old buildings with lots of other people. It was frightening and very scary for me. I knew it wasn't my place to stay here, so I managed to get myself to Germany. There I stayed for 6 months.

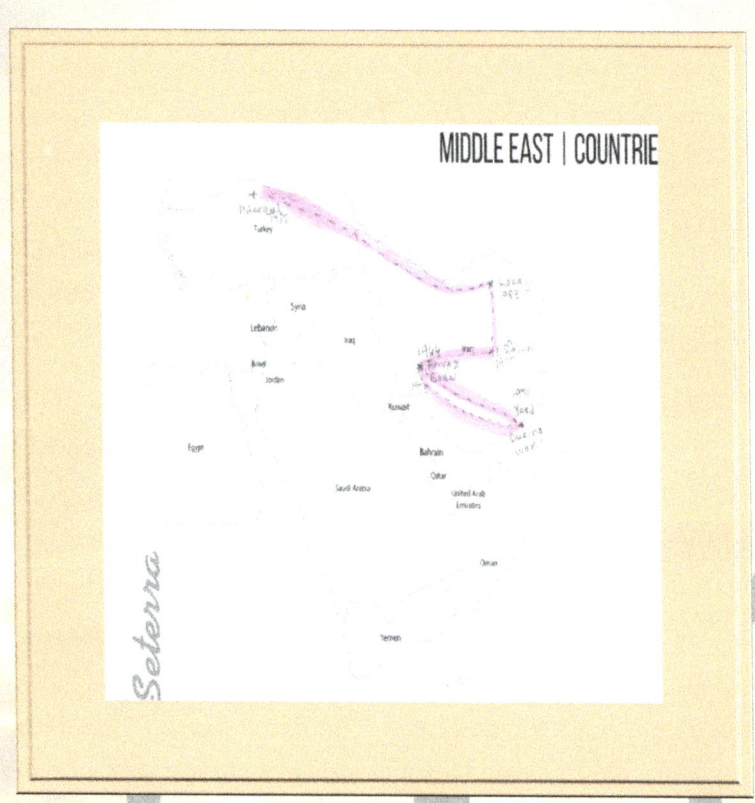

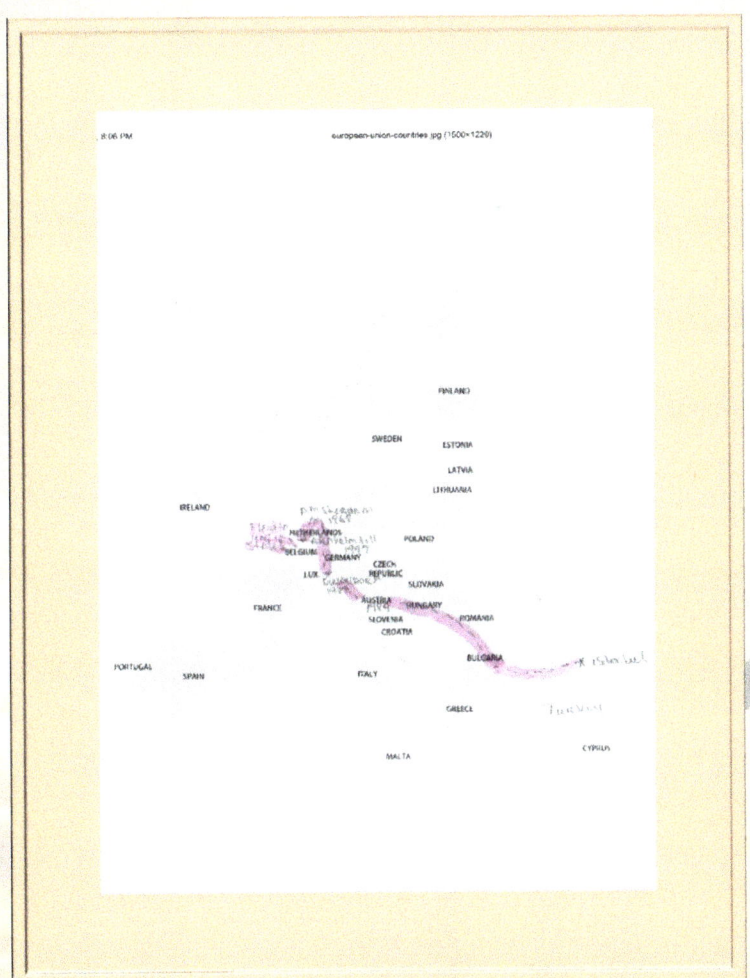

From there, I found my way to Holland by train. I again became a refugee in Holland. It was a big camp with lots of people from many different countries, including men and women from Iran. When I was in Iran, I never drank beer or any alcoholic products. I never had a girlfriend, or even knew what the woman's sexual areas looked like. I easily could have had an Iranian girlfriend. I was a very good-looking man, but I could feel that there was a force telling me, this is not your time right now. I had a guitar at that time, and I felt I still needed to be alone by myself and play the guitar. I still could feel that negative energy, which wanted me to stay living in the past; that feeling was still with me and trying to hunt me. I was tired and exhausted from that energy most of the time.

A week after being in that camp, something took me straight to a person, a force that I could not explain; I had never met or talked to that person before, and I didn't know where that person was from. When I went to this gentleman, he started talking to me, and then he started talking about Jesus in my native language, Farsi. I found out he was a Christian Iranian; his English was perfect. I never met a Christian person before in my life. I started feeling very peaceful and comfortable with this person; his name was Stephen S. He talked to me about Jesus and the bible; it was all new to me, and Stephen knew everything about the bible and Jesus. I could feel peace in myself and my soul.

A couple of days after that meeting with Stephen, when I was walking in that beautiful city, I saw a church. I went inside. It was my first time in a church. There was only one person in that big church. I saw a piano and in English I asked that gentleman if I could play some piano, he said sure, any time I

14

could come here and play piano. Then he left the church, I was all alone in that church by myself. I could feel peace and security in my soul, especially when I was playing piano. I still can remember feeling that energy or something was telling me I needed to pursue this comfortable and peaceful feeling.

I went back to Stephen and talked more with him about Jesus and Christianity, and he was very eager and patient with me, especially talking about the bible. I ended up in a Baptist church after two weeks or so, and I got baptized in that church. I could feel new life and happiness in me.

I had some Dutch, British family friends and also some American. I only remember their names, Dave and Christian, Walter and Nancy, a couple from England. We sometimes had bible studies and then would have dinners together. I also met a Dutch gentleman, Garrett (a very nice older man), and his daughter. After a few times meeting with Garrett, I remember he told me when his dad passed away, he was at his bedside and saw his dad's spirit in light separated from his body, and it went up until it disappeared.

The camp, after six months, moved me to another city called Enscheda, in Holland. After some months, the government moved me to Arnhem, also in Holland, close to where Stephen lived. There was an office in which the refugee case workers were working. I met a gentleman there he was interesting to talk to. His name was Arie Abbink. I felt like there was a connection between me and Arie. He was a strong Christian man with his wife, Joni, from Surinam. We became close friends.

I also started working, delivering newspapers in cold,

snowy early mornings on a bicycle, then later with a small motorcycle. I also worked in a milk factory at the same time. I was saving a lot of money and found a pretty girlfriend.

After a couple of years of saving, Stephen knew I had been saving my money; he told me there was a pizza business for sale if I would like to buy it. We went inside, and I saw it was busy and was making good money. I became interested in buying the business from an Afghani family. I learned many things about that business; I was eager for Stephen and me to run it. I could feel it; it was a gift from Jesus. I was very happy.

After a few weeks, I bought that business, but Stephen for some reasons could not help me, I ended up alone running that business with some pizza deliverers. It was very hard. I couldn't do it alone without family around. Arie would sometimes help me, but it still wasn't enough. At the same time, that negative energy that I was talking about before would come over me, taking my energy away from me, making it hard to function, like it was fighting with me wanting me to give up the business and not continue. So finally, the negative energy won, and after a while, I ended up selling the business.

I was thinking, "What do I do now?" I started feeling like I couldn't be alone anymore. I had some uncles living in the United States, and I wanted to visit them. So, I called my uncle in Seattle, Washington, and he invited me to come to the U.S. I flew to Seattle, and it was beautiful—I loved the United States. I knew then that I had to move here.

I went back to Holland, took care of my business, sold my things, or gave them away, and moved to the United States with only the cash I had from selling my pizza business. I ended up working in a restaurant and doing home remodeling, earning just $7 an hour. I worked hard, but that negative energy continued to follow me, weighing me down. I tried attending a couple of different churches, but nothing seemed to change.

Then one day, something came to mind: "You need to survive." I remembered I had another uncle in Tampa, Florida, who I had never met before. At that point, I had around $30,000 in cash from selling my business in Holland and a year of working hard jobs in Seattle. I called him, and he said he would help me. The only problem was that I had no green card, my Dutch visa had expired, and all I had was a U.S. driver's license. This was in 1997, and my English wasn't that good. I didn't even know what a social security number was back then.

I moved to Tampa to see how this uncle could help me. When he picked me up from the airport, I noticed he seemed like he'd been drinking. I was just hoping we'd make it to his house safely. I called him "Uncle," but he told me not to call him that, just to use his name. I asked him how he planned to help me, given that I didn't have a green card. He reassured me, saying, "Don't worry, I've got your back." He told me he was a millionaire and had a successful business, so I trusted him.

A week later, he got me a job at his best friend's company, working as a technician in some kind of field engineering role. His friend had just opened a small branch in Tampa. Again, I reminded him I didn't have a green card, and again, he said, "Don't worry, it'll be fine." So, I started working. But I still felt that negative energy of fear following me. While I was working, I kept receiving payroll papers with my uncle's name and information, including healthcare details. With my limited English, I could barely understand the papers, but I realized that I was just being used as a worker under his name.

All the while, I had $30,000 in cash—my entire life savings—sitting in my suitcase at his house. I was constantly worried about what would happen if the money got lost. I couldn't open a bank account without a green card, so I thought, "Since he's rich and successful, I'll ask him to hold onto it for me." I told him about my cash and asked if he could keep it in his bank account until I got a green card, and he agreed. So, I gave him all my money.

I worked 10 to 15 hours a day in the dark, heat, and rain of Tampa. Most days, I had to walk three hours back and forth to work because I didn't have a car. I kept receiving payroll papers but no actual money. After six months, the company moved me to their main office in Atlanta, Georgia. I had no money in my pockets, and I was working 15 to 17 hours a day, often with no sleep, in the scorching heat and freezing cold of Atlanta. I was frequently starving and thirsty, sometimes sick with allergies, especially during pollen season. I begged my uncle to send me money for food, but he told me to go ask someone from his family who worked for the company to give me $300. I did, but that money ran out quickly.

This continued for another year and a half. Finally, I called my uncle and asked for my money back. He said he had lost everything. I reminded him that he had told me he was rich and successful. I was devastated. He told me not to worry, that he would find a job and pay me back every cent. Then, he moved to California to be near another uncle and started working at a car dealership. But all my money—everything from Holland and the two years I worked in the U.S.—was gone. I had nothing.

I had no choice but to continue working under his name for another six months. The last time I called him, I was crying on the phone, and he simply hung up. I fell into deep depression, haunted by dark memories from my past.

One day, I confided in my boss, who was a distant family member. He told me he knew what my uncle had been doing and said he could help me get a green card. He introduced me to his wife's sister, who was interested in me. We got married, and she helped me get a work permit, so I could finally work legally in the U.S. She lived three hours away, and we saw each other occasionally. But after a year, she wanted a divorce. I wasn't able to connect with her due to the trauma from my past. Respectfully, I agreed to the divorce.

When we divorced, immigration sent me a letter for an interview. I went with nothing to show, and since I was divorced, they didn't issue the green card. Once again, I was back to square one.

Despite all this, I managed to buy my first house and change jobs, starting work as a concrete pump operator for Pioneer in Atlanta. I made good money, around $75,000 to $90,000 a year. But the dark side of my past still weighed heavily on me. I attended Hebron Church in Duluth, Georgia, where I made many friends. They gave me the nickname "Jam." There was one woman who was very interested in me—much younger and very pretty—but I wasn't sure about getting into a relationship.

One day, a friend brought a woman to a church event, and I noticed her immediately. We talked briefly, and before she left, something pushed me to ask for her number. A week later, I called her, and we had a great conversation. She invited me to her home. She was very kind, but her daughter wasn't so friendly. I wasn't sure about continuing the relationship because of her daughter's attitude, but we fell in love despite it.

After seven months, she asked me to marry her, and we did. She sold her house and moved in with her daughter. But her daughter remained a big problem, and I didn't know how to handle it. A friend even warned me that her daughter might destroy our marriage.

We got married in Jacksonville in 2004, and on the way back, she said, "It feels like I've won the lottery." I didn't know what she meant at the time. I took them to my church, Hebron, a few times, but my wife didn't like it. We tried other churches, but nothing seemed to satisfy her. Eventually, I gave up trying to get her to go to church.

In 2006, my beautiful son Elijah was born. But shortly after, I needed to renew my CDL license. When I went to the DMV, the clerk told me I needed a green card and other documents. It was a shock—I still didn't have a green card. I had been so busy with my family and haunted by my past that I hadn't taken care of it. Without a license, I had to quit my job, the one I loved.

It was one of the darkest moments of my life. I felt torn, unsure of what to do, but when I looked at my baby son, I knew

I had to keep going. I gave notice and quit my job, staying home while my wife went to work.

While I was holding my baby Elijah, I was crying at the same time. I had around $90,000 in cash in my bank account from pumping concrete. I paid off the house to make sure that if something happened to me, my wife would have a place to live without a mortgage. I stayed home, took care of my baby, cooked, and paid the bills. At the same time, I filed for a green card with an attorney, which I finally got after a few years.

In 2008, the economy went down, and my wife suggested we buy a foreclosure house. We looked around with an agent and found one, which we bought for $60,000. I spent $30,000 and worked for six months on it to get it ready for resale. I put it on the market, but it wouldn't sell for the price we wanted. We decided to move into this house, and I rented out the first house.

I then started buying professional broken or functional keyboard workstations on eBay or Craigslist for cheap. I would fix them and resell them back on Craigslist or eBay. I was doing very well.

In 2010, I bought a third, bigger foreclosure house. We moved into the third house. I had three paid-off houses: a primary home and two rentals. I was buying and repairing the most professional keyboards in the world. I was doing very, very well.

I was a person who, most of the time, stayed home. I didn't have many friends—maybe a few—but I liked to be by myself. I was mostly focused on my marriage and business, not on the outside world. Then, I was introduced to a man, and we became friends. That person introduced me to more friends, and all of a sudden, I found myself surrounded by a bunch of friends because I was a musician.

I had a good Christian Spanish friend that I met when I sold him several keyboards. His name was Otto. One day, Otto looked into my face and said, "JAM, THE LORD WANTS YOU TO COME TO HIM." I heard what he told me, but I didn't exactly understand what he meant. I just discarded it and forgot what he told me.

I was living a different lifestyle. I didn't know that most of my friends were the wrong kind of friends, that they were jealous of my life. They were interfering in my life in negative ways. I was so busy working, making lots of money from dealing with the keyboards, managing two rental houses, and taking care of my son. I thought my marriage was okay—until it was too late. The marriage was gradually falling apart day by day. My wife filed for divorce in 2016. It was another very dark moment in my life. Her first marriage had only lasted six months; her marriage with me lasted 14 years.

I did almost all the cooking, cleaned the houses, took her to restaurants often, paid all the bills, paid off all the houses, and dealt with all the tenants. She had nice cars, and I even helped her pay off the last car she had during our marriage. Then I ended up in front of two attorneys and a mediator in court. My attorney knew her attorney, and they had me backed into a corner—they knew exactly what they were doing. They already had a plan. They made me pay $210,000 to her, which I didn't have. I had to take out a mortgage loan on the paid-off primary house. Everything was going down the drain for me.

I had to get a loan, borrowing another $32,000 from a family member. To make a long story short, I got her that money, and she left the house that I had bought her. This was the darkest time of my life.

Why didn't I fight for my only son? I didn't have the strength to take care of him like before. After she left, I started smoking a pack of cigarettes a day, pacing back and forth, talking to myself about the past. I would finish one cigarette right after another. I didn't want to eat or drink water. The dark past that haunted me and the cigarettes were all that mattered to me—I had lost everything. I didn't want to do anything else but pace back and forth, smoke, and think of the past.

One day, I went and got a gun for the first time in my life. All I wanted to do was end it. I had never liked guns until after the divorce.

I also had around $50,000 in cash in the house; it had taken me years to save it. But something—a dark energy—made me burn that money. And I don't just mean spend it. I mean, I took gasoline and lit it on fire—the money I had worked so hard for. It wasn't me burning that money; it was that dark energy taking over my soul, and I was surrendering to it. The dark energy would take me to the dark past—pacing, talking to myself about the past, contemplating suicide, and burning money. I would start burning the money, stop, then start again. I started by burning a $1 bill to see how it would feel or look. I actually did it.

I kept thinking about my son—he was with me one day and with her the next. I could have asked my son, my neighbors, or even my friends for help—to stop me from burning the money—but I didn't. That negative energy kept me from asking for help. For at least two months, I was busy trying to burn the money in my own home. I didn't know I was surrounded by this negative energy. I was so far on the dark side that I kept all the lights in the house off. This dark energy took me into a dark closet. I was sleeping and living inside the closet. The whole house was dark. I didn't want any lights on.

I also tried to kill myself again. I had some ties that I tried to use to hang myself and suffocate. I did it several times. I could feel my heartbeat slowing and fading. Sometimes I could hear my last heartbeat and last breath while I was inside the dark closet. I was saddened that my son saw me sleeping in the closet most of the time. But in the end, thoughts of my son would come to mind, and I would save myself from death.

I loved the thought of dying and not coming back to this world. But thinking about my son would bring me back to life. I still had the money, but that negative energy still wanted me to burn it. It took me about two months to burn all of it. I spent that time thinking about nothing but burning money, reliving the dark past, smoking, and contemplating suicide. Then I would think about my son, who had lain on my chest when he was a baby and was always near me. My son—what could I do about my son? He was my world!

This was my daily routine for the next couple of months. I didn't want to do anything else. I wasn't crazy—I was a successful man. I was a musician, playing guitar and piano, a landlord, dealing with the most professional keyboards, especially Korg, Roland, and Yamaha, and I had a family. But after all those defeats in my life, my world changed to darkness. I was totally lost in the darkness and this big world.

So every day and night, I was trying to burn up that cash—$50,000. What was I thinking? I was exhausted. Finally, one day, I grabbed a small red gas can for my lawn mower that had a little gas in it. I had the money in the downstairs hallway in a big cooking pan. I picked up the gas can and looked at the cash in the pan. That dark past—negative energy—forced my right hand, holding the gas can, to dump gas on the money. I used a cigarette lighter to set it on fire. All of a sudden, I saw with my own eyes the stacks of $100 bills burning. Very quickly, I moved the big pan out of the house and onto the back porch. I put cardboard around it to make sure none of the neighbors could see it. All that money burned in just four minutes. I was crying and saying, "Elijah, I am so sorry." I knew after burning the money that I was dead. I had no desire to live anymore. I became so thin—about 100 pounds—with a dark complexion because of smoking all those cigarettes. I thought that if I stayed alive, these memories would haunt me for the rest of my life.

After the money was gone, I went back to the closet, thinking of how to end my life. I also tried to cut my arteries on my foot to let the blood flow out and slowly die, but it was hard and painful. So I tried again to hang myself in the closet. I was in deep darkness. I didn't want to deal with the rental houses anymore. I had no physical or mental strength to continue my life. I couldn't kill myself with a gun, by hanging, or any other way, but I kept thinking about how to end it. I regretted burning all that money. I could have paid off the house with it, given some to my son, helped the homeless, or started a new business—but it was too late.

A week later, that negative energy made me get rid of the houses. I called my agent, Regina A., to sell them, no matter what condition they were in. She asked me where I was going to live, and I told her in my car—I couldn't take it anymore. I was in deep pain. She told me I couldn't take my son to live with me in the car, but I told her I had to sell the houses. I begged her to sell them as quickly as possible. She did sell them very fast. At the same time, I got rid of everything in the house—sold some or gave things away for free, things that had taken me years to collect. I was still trying to kill myself, and I wanted to give the money from the sale of the houses to my son. But there was another force, another energy, telling me that there might still be some hope left. It was the first time I felt it. I was afraid of the world and everything in it; everything I had worked for my whole life was taken from me once again. I was treated so badly. The positive and negative energies were pulling me in every direction.

After I sold the houses, I didn't know where to go. I kept asking myself, "Why did you get rid of those houses?" It was like the burning of the money—too late. I decided to move to California to stay with one of my uncles. I knew the negative energy was still after me, and I felt like it wasn't done with me yet. I had a little bit of my stuff left, so I rented a U-Haul, packed everything into the car and U-Haul, and headed toward California, hoping to leave that negative energy behind me.

I turned on the radio, and Christian music was playing, but for some reason, I felt compelled to turn it off. I was in New Mexico, and just a few minutes before I was going to take an exit to get some rest, I took one of the sleeping pills I had left. By the time I reached the exit, I started to fall asleep behind the wheel. Suddenly, I couldn't see anything in front of me. The sky turned dark even though it was early evening. I couldn't understand how, in just a few minutes after taking the pill, I was in such a deep sleep. That had never happened to me before.

There was traffic ahead of me on the road, but I couldn't see anything. I reached the end of the exit, very close to a main road, but by then, I was completely asleep behind the wheel. The next thing I knew, two police officers were waking me up. The engine of the car was still running. When I looked around, I saw a big Ford truck tipped over in a ditch, right in front of my car. I asked the officer, "What is this?" He said, "You don't know what this is? You did this!" They asked if I had been drinking or using drugs, and I told them I had taken a sleeping pill. They saw the bottle near my car door. They took me out of the car, handcuffed me, and brought me to the hospital. After running blood tests, they took me to jail.

I remember the jail being about a mile from where the accident had occurred. It was in the middle of nowhere. I couldn't believe it—my first time ever in jail. I could hear other men screaming from their cells. The food smelled terrible, and I didn't want to eat most of the time. I only drank water. While I was there, the dark memories of my past wouldn't let me go. They pulled me in every direction.

I stayed in jail for a week. Eventually, they called me, gave me some papers to sign, and told me I could leave. They said I needed to get an attorney for the accident. They also told me where my car was. After leaving the jail, I walked about a mile and found my car at a small tow company. I spoke to the man there and saw the truck that had ended up in the ditch. It was completely destroyed. I asked him how the accident had happened. He explained that when I fell asleep behind the wheel, my car and the U-Haul stopped in the middle of the intersection. The truck, which was going fast, saw my car too late. The driver swerved to avoid hitting my car, lost control, and flipped into the ditch. The man told me the driver would be coming after me for damages.

I paid the tow fees, got my car, and continued to California. When I finally arrived at my uncle's house, I was still in my pajamas, and I didn't look good at all. I was very skinny, and my face was dark. My family could see that I wasn't in a good place; I was living in the past. I paced back and forth constantly and had no appetite, but they insisted I eat. After a couple of weeks, they couldn't handle my unusual behavior anymore. I wasn't the same person they knew. The dark energy was still with me, whether I was inside or outside. I was still thinking about suicide.

My son was on my mind most of the time. He was my world. I decided to leave and return to Georgia, buy a small house, and start over. I needed to take care of my son again. I left my family and went back to Georgia. When I got to Atlanta, I asked a friend who was a cabinet builder if I could stay in his warehouse until I found a house.

Then I heard that my ex had gotten married and that my son was living with another man. It tore my heart out. I also found out that her new husband's house was in Lawrenceville, Georgia—where all my previous houses had been. I asked a friend's wife, who was a real estate agent, to help me find a small house. She recommended I buy something around $250,000, as it would be a better investment. I listened to her, and she found me a big house, almost 3,000 square feet, with a long backyard. It was a nice house, so I bought it. It wasn't far from where my son was living with her new husband.

Right after I bought the house, I got new furniture and started from scratch. I sent my ex the address to make sure the school bus would bring my son to my house. Ten minutes later, she texted back, saying the address wasn't in my son's school district, so the school bus wouldn't stop there. I was devastated. The house was only a block away from her new husband's place, and it felt like another nightmare had come upon me. I decided to put the house back on the market.

Next, I needed a job. I worked for a friend for four months, picking up heavy kitchen cabinets, but the drive from the house was too far. I had to sleep in his warehouse most of the time, next to his dog. He paid me $2,000, but he still owed me another $2,000. I was shocked. This was someone I had helped so much while I was married. Then I called my previous boss to see if I could work as a concrete pump operator again, like I had years ago. I got the job, but it was also too far to drive back and forth, so I slept in my car most of the time. My boss was happy to have me back, but he could see I wasn't in a good place, always pacing and talking about the past. He finally told me it was too risky to have me on the team, and after six months, he let me go.

I found another job closer to the house, doing the same kind of work, but I was in so much emotional pain, and the dark thoughts from my past haunted me. After seven months, I

29

couldn't handle life anymore. I stopped going to work. I was exhausted—emotionally and spiritually. I was separated from my son, and I had no idea where my life was headed.

After quitting work, I went to a nearby gas station to buy a pack of cigarettes. I saw a woman standing outside. For some reason, I started talking to her about my life and my past. She told me she was a good person, always trying to help people, and that she never stole anything. I must have been vulnerable, because I gave her my phone number—something I never do with strangers. You'll see why. An hour later, she called and said she needed help. She told me she lived with a friend, but he had hit her and didn't treat her well. She asked if she could stay with me for a little while. I told her I could help.

I went to pick her up and helped her pack all her belongings, along with her six cats, into my car. I brought her to my home and told her she could stay in one of the empty rooms. She said she preferred to stay in my garage, and I told her that was fine. Then she asked if she could use my address to get an ID card. I said no. Later, I found out she had gone through my bills and gotten the information she needed to get the ID anyway.

After a few days, I noticed some of my belongings were missing from the house. I suspected this had something to do with the woman I had taken in. I asked her where my missing items were, and she insisted she didn't steal anything. However, she began to speak too fast and loudly. A few days later, I noticed more things were gone.

I called a friend about the situation, and he advised me to kick her out of the house as soon as possible. He wanted to meet her, and when he did, he told me, "Jam, as soon as I looked into her eyes, I saw the devil inside them! This is not good; you need to kick her out immediately." At that moment, I began to understand what was happening in my life. The dark, negative energy that had followed me for so long had finally manifested in this woman, who had been waiting for the right moment to invade my space.

I confronted her, telling her she was the devil and needed to leave my home. She replied, "Jam, I know everything about you—your past and your future. I know who you are, and you have no idea whom you're dealing with. I will follow you until I bring you down." I didn't fully understand what she meant, but I thought to myself, "Why me?" I realized that she had no true identity, just as we know the devil has no identity.

During this time, I called my son to check on him, and he told me he and his mother had moved to Jacksonville, Florida. She had divorced her husband; this was her third divorce, and her third marriage had lasted only six months. I heard she received some money from her ex-husband during that brief period.

I shared this information with the woman who had taken refuge in my home, mentioning my son and his mother. She suggested it would be better for me to follow my son to Jacksonville. At that moment, I knew this woman would pursue me wherever I went. But again, I asked myself, "Why me?"

A few days later, one of her cats wandered into my neighbor's backyard. I told her we should go retrieve the cat, but she looked at me angrily and said no, that she didn't want them to see her. I wondered why she felt that way. Eventually,

I learned that my neighbor belonged to a strong Christian family. If they looked into her eyes, they would see the devil within her, which is why she didn't want to be seen.

I reiterated to the woman that she needed to leave my house soon and went upstairs to my room. Suddenly, I heard screaming downstairs. When I rushed down, I found her sitting on the living room floor, praying in a strange, almost satanic manner. I realized she was cursing the house and me. She thrived on my anxiety and my past, seemingly hoping to drive me to despair.

The next day, I called the police about the situation. When they arrived, they asked her questions, but she continued to speak too quickly and loudly, acting unusually. The police instructed her to calm down, but she persisted in her erratic behavior. They told her she had to leave the house either that day or the next. As they left, she warned me that she would follow me wherever I went until she brought me down. I found myself asking again what she wanted from me. I had only brought her in to help.

While she was still in the house, I went to the store to buy some food. When I returned, she told me that a friend was coming to pick her up with all her belongings. Shortly after, her friend arrived and took her away. Once they left, I discovered that most of my kitchen items were missing.

A day later, she called, saying she had left one of her cats inside the house and asked if she could come to retrieve it. I told her I didn't see any cat, but I allowed her to come and look for it. She returned with her friend around 8 p.m. Her friend kept me occupied outside, and I heard her calling for the cat while she went upstairs. A few minutes later, she emerged, and I noticed something inside her closed jacket. I assumed it was her cat. She told her friend they should leave, and they hurried away.

As soon as they left, I went into my closet and discovered that all my important documents—tax documents, my passport, and some cash—were gone from my suitcase and jacket. I understood now why they had left in such a rush. I called the police again, and they came to take a report, but they had no leads on her and could not take further action. A month later, I sold the house and decided to move to Jacksonville, only because of my son.

When I got there, I called my ex-sister-in-law. I told her I knew nothing about Jacksonville and didn't know where to go when I arrived. I was only coming there for my kid. I put the remainder of my belongings in my car, left Georgia, and headed to Jacksonville, Florida. I had no idea where to go in such a big city. It was hot, and I had to sleep in my car. Sometimes I got to see my son, but I was overwhelmed with thoughts about how to start a new life in this unfamiliar place. I had no friends here and felt very confused.

In the first couple of months in Jacksonville, I was scared and lost. One night, I stopped at a gas station around 9 PM, pacing back and forth while smoking cigarettes, spiraling back into my dark past. Suddenly, a car pulled up next to mine. It was an older Honda, and the driver was reading his Bible in his car. Something compelled me to approach him, and I started talking about my struggles. He told me he normally didn't come to that gas station, but something divine urged him to stop and give me a message. He said, "Do not go to the past, or they won't let you go. They will chase you and bring you down."

I asked him, "Who are they?" He replied, "The devil. I see them all around you." He added, "If you go to the past, they will take even more from you." I mentioned the $50,000 cash I had burned in my house after the divorce and how I felt I had lost everything because of cigarettes. He looked me in the eye and said, "NO. Do not go to the past. You lost everything not because of cigarettes, but because of YOU. Again, do not go to the past." He moved closer to his car, began reading his Bible again, and left after about 20 minutes. I never saw him again, and I regretted not following him to safety.

A week later, I visited my ex-brother-in-law. When he found out I had $360,000 cash in my bank account, he advised me to invest in Ford stock. This was around the time the coronavirus hit the country, and the economy, including the stock market, was plummeting in March 2020. I listened to him and invested all my money in stocks. As soon as I bought Ford stock, my investments dropped. After a couple of months, the stock prices rose, and I made some money. During this time, I was living in my ex-brother-in-law's camper, which was hot, dirty, and infested with large mosquitoes. I had no clean water and felt utterly confused. I was literally living in hell. The dark past and the negative energy still haunted me. I knew it was the devil pursuing me, but I didn't understand why. I could barely cope; it was too much to handle.

Then that devil woman called. She asked, "Where are you?" I replied, "I'm in Jacksonville. What do you want from me?"

She said, "I brought you into my house to help you, but you stole everything from me," and then she hung up. This was in April 2020.

I didn't know how or where to start my new life from scratch in this big, hot city. I thought I needed to find a trucking company job, but first, I needed a CDL Class A commercial driving license. I called several CDL schools and left messages. A woman from CRST Trucking Company called me, saying she could get me the CDL within three weeks, but I would need to go to Iowa. She said she would make arrangements within the next two days, and I would be traveling to Iowa with two other students in a rental car. I agreed.

The next morning, a Christian friend called me and said, "Jam, Joshua from the Bible came to me in a dream and told me to tell you to stay very strong." I heard his message but didn't fully understand it.

Then I sold my car, though I wasn't sure why. A few days later, the two other CDL students arrived with a rental car to pick me up, along with my six bags containing all my personal belongings. We headed toward Iowa, which would take 23 hours. Each person had to drive for 7 to 8 hours. I was the last driver. I was obeying the speed limit, but due to my poor state of mind, I briefly exceeded it and got pulled over by the police, receiving a ticket. I continued driving toward Iowa and finally arrived at the CDL school, which also served as a hotel.

As soon as I entered my room, I called my recruiter to explain what had happened on the drive—I had received a speeding ticket. She immediately told me that because of the ticket, I couldn't attend the school. I asked her for a bus ticket back to Jacksonville, but she said I should wait for her to call me back. In the meantime, I figured it might be better to trade stocks with the money I had while waiting. I bought Carnival stock, but right after I purchased it, the price dropped. In one day, I lost around $100,000. I then tried investing in Dave & Buster's stock, but the same thing happened; I lost a significant amount of money. I couldn't believe it—every time I bought stocks, they dropped, and as soon as I sold them, they went back up. Now, I had about $250,000 left.

The CDL recruiter called me back, saying they would get me a bus ticket to Jacksonville. I got my ticket, boarded the bus, and headed south. After an hour on the bus, I looked at my ticket and realized it was for Atlanta, Georgia (where I had lost everything), not Jacksonville (where my son was). I panicked, wondering where I would go once I reached Atlanta. After a day, we arrived in Atlanta at night, and it was cold. I called Otto (the same Christian friend who had encouraged me to seek the Lord during my marriage). I told him I needed a place to stay. He said he would call his pastor to see if I could stay at their Spanish church. This was in May 2020.

He called me back, saying he had secured permission for me to stay at the church. Otto picked me up, and as we drove, he told me about a preacher—a Black man who stayed at the church. He had arrived in January 2020. When we got to the church, I saw the preacher sleeping on a piece of soundproof foam right in front of the altar. There was only one light on in the whole place, shining directly on the pastor's head.

Otto told me, "Jam, kneel down and pray." I knelt and

prayed with him. After he left the church, I found some chairs and slept.

When I woke up in the morning, I saw the preacher walking back and forth, praying, pointing his finger, and talking to someone, but I didn't see anyone around him. I introduced myself and asked about him. He said his name was Peter Brocks and that he was American. I asked him what he was doing in a Spanish church, and he told me he had been preaching in Guatemala last December. The Lord told him to go back to the United States. I asked why he was at a Spanish church, and he said the Lord told him to come and stay there. Then he said, "I came all the way to this church only for one individual, to change one individual's life." I asked him who that individual was, and he pointed at me and said, "YOU!"

I was shocked and felt a wave of numbness wash over me. I wondered what was happening and why I had come to this church. I told Peter, "I don't understand. I left Jacksonville to get a CDL; I could have gotten my CDL right there. I didn't need to go all the way to Iowa just for that. I had a car, but I sold it for reasons I still don't understand! I got a speeding ticket on the way to Iowa, which is why I couldn't attend the CDL school!"

Peter replied, "IT WAS ALL SET UP FOR YOU TO GET HERE IN THIS CHURCH." I was shocked again, feeling numb all over. I still didn't know what was happening in my life.

I realized he was right—if I hadn't received that speeding ticket, I would have ended up working for that CRST trucking company in Iowa and would never have reached this church or met this man. I asked Peter, "Who are you?"Then he started telling me his life story. He said that in 1993, he had a wife, kids, a house, and an excellent job as a Domino's Pizza manager, making $150,000 a year. While attending church, one Sunday, Jesus touched him. Right after that, he knelt on the ground with tears in his eyes. Peter said he heard the most precious voice of his life. He said, "Jesus told me, 'Peter, if you continue your life like this, you will go backward, but if you follow me, you will go forward.'" He added that while he would have loved to see Jesus's face, he couldn't. That was all Peter shared with me at the time, but I am sure Jesus told him more—Peter just didn't disclose everything.

Peter said he then started attending church more frequently and focused on the Bible, but his wife didn't like it. One day, his wife told him, "Peter, if you keep living like this, you will lose your family." For a while, he didn't know what to choose—Jesus or his family. He eventually chose Jesus. He got a divorce, losing his wife, house, and excellent job. He said to me, "Jam, you have no idea how I've been living these past seven years. I've lived in dirty, cold mechanic shops and various churches. It's been tough." All he had was a light sky-blue BMW and a thick Bible.

I noticed a wedding ring on his finger and asked, "Why do you still wear a wedding ring if you're divorced?" He replied, "Yes, I'm divorced, but I'm married to Jesus."

I could sense that I was very important to Peter, but I didn't know why. He was always trying to teach me good things, often telling me, "The Lord said, 'Peter, stay clean,'" or he would say, "The Lord authorized me." I didn't understand what he meant by that. Peter knew the Bible inside and out—if I asked him a question, he would answer with the exact words from the Bible. I knew it wasn't easy to memorize those verses, something I certainly couldn't do.

In the evenings, when I lay on the chairs, I could see and hear him walking around, talking to someone, and pointing at something invisible. I'd also hear loud noises, like explosions or fire, but nothing was there. Sometimes, Peter would tell me he could see fire outside the church doors, and that "they" were trying to get inside. When I asked who was trying to get in, he said, "The demons." When I asked why I couldn't see them, he replied, "With the power of the Holy Spirit, you can see them."

This reminded me of the man at the gas station in Jacksonville with the Honda, who had told me not to dwell on the past, as he could see demons all around me. I asked him who "they" were, and he had also said, "The demons."

Peter often spoke in parables, just like Jesus did. Sometimes, I didn't understand what he meant, and I had to ask him to speak more plainly. He also wore a white scarf with the name of my son, "Elijah," embroidered on it. It was beautiful. I asked Peter, "Why do you have my son's name on your scarf?" He said, "The Lord told me to put it on." I started crying, with tears streaming down my face, and a numb feeling washed over me.

I kept asking myself, "What's going on? Why did Peter come all the way from Guatemala to this church, just months before I got here?" A few weeks later, I asked the church members when Peter had arrived, and they told me he had come in January 2020. This matched what Peter and Otto had told me.

Though Peter was an American, I heard him speak Farsi—my native language. I was shocked. I asked him how he could speak Farsi, and he said it was the Holy Spirit. That's when I learned he spoke in tongues.

Peter loved children, just like Jesus did. One day, after a service, he gathered some children around him. I was close by and overheard him tell them, "You will all have a dream in the next few nights, but don't tell anyone." A week later, the children returned to the church with their parents. Peter asked them, "Did you have that dream a few nights ago?" The children, excited, said, "Yes!" Peter replied, "Don't tell anyone."

Jesus was Peter's life—his everything. He didn't care about money, and everything he did was for Jesus.

One time, I was outside the church and asked someone for a cigarette. Peter saw me and said, "Jam, don't smoke. Your body is the temple of the Holy Spirit. Is nicotine more important to you than Jesus?" At the time, I wasn't sure what he meant.

As you know, I am a musician. One Sunday, I saw young kids playing the piano, guitar, drums, and singing during the service. I started crying, thinking about how I hadn't taught my son any musical instruments. As I cried, I left the church. Peter noticed and followed me out. He said, "Jam, let's go get some coffee." While driving, he said, "The Lord wants you to come to Him," and again started speaking in parables, which I struggled to understand. We spent about 30 minutes at a restaurant, drinking coffee. He continued to share things from the Bible, but I wasn't spiritually ready to receive them. Afterward, we returned to the church.

Peter knew I had some money in the bank and that I was trading stocks. I asked him, "Why do all my stocks drop right after I buy them? I've lost a lot of money." Then he said, "Answer this question honestly, Jam. What would you do if you had $1 million in your account?" I replied, "I would go back to Jacksonville, buy a house, and take care of my son. I'd also help the poor and homeless." Peter then said, "It won't happen right now."

I started trading stocks inside or around the church. I could tell he didn't like what I was doing; every stock I bought would drop. I noticed he was often looking at his phone, and I asked him, "Why do all my stocks go down right after I buy them, and go back up after I sell?" He replied, "Things change because you don't read the Bible often enough, and you don't raise your hands when you pray. Is this stock more important to you than Jesus?"

At that moment, I knew it was him who was lowering my stocks, simply by looking at his phone—without even asking me what stocks I had. I realized he had the power to do that. I remembered that several times he had told me, "The Lord authorized me." I begged him, "Please raise my stocks." But he said, "Ask Jesus to raise your stocks; He is the only one who can do that."

I asked him, "Who are you? Why are you doing this to me?" He responded, "I knew you before you came here. You have no idea who you are dealing with." Again, I asked him, "Who are you?" He then said, "I am a prophet and a SEER." He asked me if I knew what a seer was. I said I didn't. He explained, "A seer is someone who can see the future. I can see behind a thick concrete wall." I asked him, "How can you see behind a concrete wall?" He replied, "With the Holy Spirit."

One day, he proved to me that he could see behind a concrete wall. He told me about my past, about things that happened years ago in my marriage. He mentioned that I didn't have a good relationship with my ex-wife's daughter. He told me he knew everything about my past and that the devil had control over my life in the past. He also said, "Right now, all the doors are closed to you, but at the right time and place, the doors will open." He was exactly right; I could see all the doors were closed to me. I was amazed—how did he know all about my past?

I must tell the world about the power of the Holy Spirit and the power of Jesus. This is not a simple thing—a person like him telling me about my life from many years ago.

As I mentioned before, Peter had no house, job, or wife. All he had was a car. In the second week, he told me he applied for a $150,000 loan from the bank. I asked him, "How are you able to get a loan when you have nothing but a car?" He said, "I will get it; the Lord promised me that I would get the loan." After a month and a half, he got the loan—$147,000 from the bank. He showed me the bank documents.

He said, "My plan is to establish a dollar store in Guatemala. Then after three months, I'll open the second dollar store, and after another three months, the third dollar store. I will have many dollar stores in several different countries, and then I'll become the U.S. President. The Lord will get me into that position." He continued, "Many CEOs will stand before me, but I already have the answers for them, by the power of the Holy Spirit."

I also remember one morning when Peter told me he had a dream that Russia would attack the United States.

After nearly four months of being around him at the church, one night, around 8 or 9 p.m., it was just Peter and me inside the church. I saw and heard him standing in front of the altar. He raised his hands strongly and prayed, "Heavenly Father, my mission is done; I am coming back home." His mission was me. Then he came over and told me, "I have blessed many people in this church, and when I leave, the people of this church will never see me again." Remember, it was the spirit inside him that would go back home, not his body.

After Peter accomplished his mission, he found a job in a dry-cleaning business in Doraville, Georgia, delivering clothes to various areas in North and South Carolina, as well as in Georgia. I went with him to North Carolina a few times. The name of the dry-cleaning business was JC Kleen. Without asking him, I figured out it stood for "Jesus Christ Kleen."

Once, when we were in South Carolina and he was driving slowly through a shopping center, he turned his face toward me and said, "People think I know nothing, but I know everything. I know the past, the present, and the future." Again, I asked him, "Who are you?" He said, "I am God." I told him, "If you are God, then let me worship you." He replied, "No, you don't worship a man; you only worship Jesus."

After that week, I left the church and Peter. I went to stay with Otto, who made me a small, tiny place inside a shed next to his rental house. It was about a 3'x4' area for me to stay in. It would get cold in there, but they offered me blankets, food, and some drinks. I stayed in that tiny spot for about a month and a half or a little longer.

One day, I became very, very sick. Otto called an ambulance, and they took me to the hospital, where I stayed for two weeks. While I was in the hospital, Peter called me. Without asking anyone, he knew where I was. He knew because of the power of the Holy Spirit in him. If you remember, he said he could see behind a thick concrete wall— he already knew where I was. He wanted to make sure I was okay, and he said, "About eight weeks ago, when I was in a hotel room after work, Jesus touched me and spoke to me. I heard the same precious voice I had heard before. I knelt down, praying and crying with tears in my eyes. Jesus assigned me to the land of Guatemala, the land of Mexico, and a few other countries in South America."

At the end, Peter said the only thing he wanted was to see Jesus's face, but he couldn't. He also told me the Lord had told him to help me. He said, "Jam, you will be fine."When I was in the hospital, I met a man that had nice vintage sunglasses on and a cowboy hat. His name was Chris. I told him he had nice sunglasses on. We started talking about our lives and jobs. I told him I needed to get CDL so I could start working. He said he has a bus with CDL, and he can help me to get my CDL, but I need to travel with him to Indiana, he lives with his girlfriend there, but he came to Georgia for his friend's wedding. He will be going back to Indiana the next week. He said, "Don't worry, I'll help you," he got my phone number and he left the hospital.

After a few days, I left the hospital. The hospital got me an Uber. I had given the hospital Otto's address, but the Uber accidentally dropped me off at a shelter in downtown Atlanta. The driver said the hospital gave him the wrong address. Then he dropped me off right there. When I looked around, I saw a shelter. There was also a church on the other side where the Uber driver dropped me off. I went inside to see what was going on, and they gave me a ticket to get in to take a shower and dinner. There were about 40 homeless people there. After everybody had taken a shower, they started serving dinner. After dinner, we all had to sit on the chairs for a short service. There were two guitarists and a preacher. After playing a few worship songs, then the preacher started his preaching. His sermon was about "the lord's free gift." He said, "You have a free gift; go get it." At that time, I didn't quite understand what he meant. But I heard what the preacher said. After the service, everybody put mattresses on the floor and went to sleep. At the same time, Chris the person that I met at the hospital, called me and said he would come to pick me up, and we would go to Indiana to stay with his girlfriend. I said Ok and went to bed. When we woke up in the morning and had some breakfast, everybody had to leave the shelter.

I left the church while I was walking on the street; then Chris from the hospital called me again and said he would come in a couple of hours to pick me up. I gave him the shelter's address. He actually came and picked me up; we went to Otto's house, got all my belongings and headed toward Indiana.

After driving for about 30 minutes, he told me," I am not supposed to be a Christian. I must be a Muslim." I told him no, I am a Christian. He was a white American; I didn't understand why he would say that to me. Then he started arguing with me and changed his attitude. He was a quiet man when I met him at the hospital, but he all of a sudden changed. I told myself I didn't need this, and I thought I was with the wrong person. Then he grabbed a bottle full of marijuana, filled up his pipe, and started smoking while he was driving. He talked so fast about nonsense stuff and driving 95 miles per hour, then zigzagging in and out of the cars. I told him, what are you doing? Are you trying to kill us? He didn't listen to me and continued smoking weed, talking too fast about nonsense stuff, and driving too fast."

I had no option because we were already a few hours on the road toward Indiana, but to make a long story short. What should have been only a day and half trip took us three days to get to Indiana. We finally got to his girlfriend's house in La Port, Indiana. It was a very bad area in that town. When we went inside the house, I saw that the house was full of trash, old, stinky, dirty, old broken furniture, and also lots of guns. It was a house built around 1850's; it had a floor house with two doors, one for downstairs and another door for upstairs. Then he told me, Jam, from now on, you are responsible for cleaning up the whole house, taking care of our dogs, mowing the yard, and more. I was thinking, after owning three houses, now I must clean up this guy's house. I came here with the wrong person. He had an argument with his girlfriend, hit her, and talked nasty to me and his girlfriend. He was smoking weed all the time. He said he owns me like a slave. His girlfriend became sick, and someone else had to take her to the hospital. Then Chris left the house, not sure where he went to.

During this time, something was pushing me to go to the DMV and prepare myself for CDL licenses. I found out where the DMV was. I walked about two miles to DVM, started getting my CDL permit, and in a couple of days, I got most of the endorsements. But I still needed the CDL itself.

In the first week, when I was inside the house, someone knocked on the door. I opened it to see three police officers standing there. They asked who I was and why I was there. I explained my situation, and they told me that someone had called the police, claiming that I had guns and drugs in my suitcases. I told them, "Not me!" and invited them to check my suitcases. They searched them and found nothing. They said the person had lied to them and warned me that I had come with the wrong people, that this wasn't a safe place for me.

The officers then took me to a Holiday Inn hotel with my belongings and gave me a phone number to call in the morning. The lady's name was Lisa. The next morning, I called Lisa, and she arranged for a cab to bring me to her office. When I arrived, she assured me that I was safe now.

After about an hour of talking, she told me that they would help me get my CDL. She then sent me to another city in Indiana with a Christian gentleman. The man took me to Michigan City, where they first administered a COVID test, and I was fine. He then brought me to a shelter called "Keys to Hope." It was a nice place, housing about 20 homeless people. It was quiet, clean, and the people were friendly and respectful. They had good showers, good food, and a good atmosphere.

Around 5 PM every day, we had to take a bus or walk to another location, an old church. After a few days of getting to know the staff and management, I learned there was another building next to the church that helped people in need. It was called Grace Center. I went there and met a lady named Erica, the manager. I told her about my interest in getting my CDL. Erica was kind and respectful, and she said she would help me. She called the CDL school and spoke with the manager, Bryan.

Bryan called me back and told me he could help me get a free government grant and that I could get my CDL in four weeks. He said he would call me once he got the approval. A few hours later, he called back and confirmed that I got the grant and could start school on Monday. I felt like doors were finally opening for me, but the only problem was getting to another city without a car.

I spoke to the manager of Keys to Hope, and he said, "Jam, you've come a long way; I know you can make it." He then showed me a lady's bicycle and suggested I ride it to the bus station, put it on the bus, and then ride it to the school once I got off.

On Monday morning, I did exactly as he instructed. When I arrived at the school, there were about six students in the classroom. During the break, I noticed a female student looking at me. She kept looking at me, and eventually, she came over and introduced herself. Her name was Ernestine. She told me she was a prophet and that she had been sent to deliver a message from the Lord. I was shocked and numb, thinking to myself, "Oh my God, another Peter!"

However, Ernestine didn't give me the message at that time.

She was a nice person. After class, she offered to drive me back to Keys to Hope, and I put my bicycle in her car. As we drove, we talked, and she took my number. When we arrived at the shelter, she dropped me off, and I went inside.

Later that evening, while I was in the old church after dinner, I received a text message from Ernestine. The message said, "I am preparing you, says the Lord. You feel like, 'Why me?' or 'How am I going to make it through? I can't take one more thing (disappointment).' God says, it's not on you but to trust in Him. When you are weak, that's when I show up strong. Trust in Me! You don't feel equipped, but I am everything you need. I am not like man; I will never leave you or forsake you. In this season, get into My Word and let it carry you. God is saying you need to focus solely on Him. The enemy wants to distract you, but the battle is already won. You are in a fixed fight."

I still have that text message, and I will never lose it. I was in tears when I texted Ernestine to thank her. She texted me back, explaining that she hadn't sent the message herself—it was from a friend of hers who was in the hospital, in pain. I was amazed, thinking, "I've never even met this woman, and she sent me such a precious message."

After four weeks, I finally earned my CDL. I began looking for trucking companies, making a list of those offering the best pay and benefits. One company that stood out was JBS, the largest meat company in the world. That caught my attention. I went to Erica at Grace Center to ask for her opinion on which company would be the best for me.

Without even looking at my list, Erica said, "Jam, go with

JBS." I decided to take her advice. I called JBS and spoke to a recruiter named Jeff. He told me they wanted me and arranged everything, even booking me a plane ticket to Green Bay, Wisconsin.

When I told the people at Keys to Hope that I was leaving, many of them were sad, and some were even crying because we had become close, and they knew they wouldn't see me again. I then went to the airport and flew to Green Bay, Wisconsin.

When I arrived at the JBS Company, they assigned me a trainer for 6 weeks. After the training, I was ready to drive by myself, but I had some doubts about the truck's computer and the ELD system, as my trainer hadn't covered that very well, especially regarding DOT regulations.

A few weeks later, while parked at a service center rest area in Ohio, the company noticed that I was still struggling with the truck's computer. I had six DOT violations. My boss called me, saying, "You have six DOT violations. Don't move the truck, not even an inch." He said he would send another driver to pick me up and bring me to the Green Bay terminal. I didn't move the truck at all. When the other driver arrived, he drove me to Green Bay, Wisconsin.

At the terminal, I went into my boss's office, where he told me I would need a few more days of training with another trainer. After the meeting, I left his office and sat down on a chair next to the main door. I noticed an older gentleman about 15 feet away looking at me, but I wasn't sure why. All of a sudden, I asked him, "Do you believe in Jesus?" He replied, "Of course." I then started talking to him about my experiences with Peter and other things. While he was listening, the man came toward me and said, "You're a very well-spoken person."

Just then, my boss came out of his office and said, "Jam, you'll be going with Dave for a few more days of training." It turned out the older man I was speaking with was Dave, my new trainer. Dave and I began the training. He was 70 years old.

One evening, while we were waiting for them to unload the truck, we sat inside Dave's truck. He shared with me that his daughter had passed away from cancer at the age of 47. She had battled the disease for the last 20 years of her life, and they were very close. She had tried several surgeries but, in the end, couldn't survive. A few years after her passing, Dave himself was diagnosed with cancer in his mouth and neck. During surgery to remove the cancerous cells, Dave died for 6 minutes.

During that time, his spirit separated from his body and ascended. He saw his daughter in heaven. She waved at him, and he waved back. As he got closer to her, they hugged. Then, he heard a powerful voice coming from within a bright light.The voice told him, "This is not your time; you must go back. You have a mission to accomplish." Then Dave's spirit descended back to his body. But, he became a different person in spirit. He also showed me his tongue and neck, where they removed parts of them. Then he told me, "Jam, I want to show you something." I said sure. He took off his shoes and his socks. I saw two nail crucifixion marks right on the middle of each foot, the same as Jesus' nail crucifixion marks on both his feet. Dave then said, if he showed them to some people, they don't believe me, I told him I believe you. It was about 45 minutes left to get to my truck, while I was sitting on the passenger seat and he was driving, Dave turned his face toward me and started talking, and I saw another person inside his face, it wasn't exactly Dave's face, it was another serious person inside his face and he told me "Jam the angels, and I have been around you for quite sometimes for your protection, you will meet the lord, the lord loves you, you have a gift, you'll become one of us. I was just looking at him, and again, I was shocked. My body went numb while I was looking and listening to him. He also said, "The lord cleansed your soul, do not dirty that soul, the lord loves you, but you need to have lots of respect for him. All your past was controlled by the devil, but your present and your future is in Lord's hands now you are on the right track." He said, "The lord chose you for this job. This way you can work and you spend time with him, continue preaching, but if somebody doesn't want to listen to you, then you leave that person behind." He also said; let's pray together, I prayed while I cried with tears running down from my eyes. He left me at my truck and he was gone.

About a day after that I called Dave to see how he's doing. He said, Jam did you see another person in me yesterday? I said, yes of course, I saw another person inside your face, a very serious person, it was not you. Then he said, the apostle's spirit comes and uses his body to communicate with people but at the end of the day he becomes very exhausted. Dave told me about the apostle's spirit, but I forgot the name.

Then Dave requested from me that I read the Ephesians in the New Testament, I was wondered why he wants me to read the Ephesians. After few days, I did read the Ephesians, but I still didn't get the point. I read the Ephesians for the second time again, in chapter one, where Paul says: "Long ago, even before (God) had made the world, God chose us to be his very own, through what Christ would do for us, he decided to make us holy in his eyes without a single fault, we who stand before him covered with his love, his unchanged plan has always been to adopt us into his own family by sending Jesus Christ to die for us. And he did this because he wanted to! And because what Christ did, for all of us who have also heard the good news about how to be saved and trusted in Christ, "WE ARE MARKED AS BELONGINGS TO CHRIST BY THE HOLY SPIRIT, and WHO LONG AGO HAD BEEN PROMISED TO ALL OF US CHRISTIANS. HIS PRESENCE WITHIN US IS GOD'S GUARANTEE THAT HE REALLY WILL GIVE US ALL THAT HE PROMISED. AND THE SPIRIT 'S SEAL UPON US MEANS THAT GOD HAS ALREADY GRANTED US THAT GUARANTEES TO BRING US TO HIMSELF. THIS IS JUST ONE MORE REASON FOR US TO PRAISE OUR GLORIOUS GOD."

We were marked as belonging to Christ by the Holy Spirit!!

This got my attention. I went online and researched more about it, and I found out amazing stuff. "THE LORD'S GIFT SEALED MARK ON OUR FOREHEAD" (THE HOLY SPIRIT). Then I read more and researched more, found out this is what Satan is after. It is what Satan tries to find and then tries to destroy that person's life. Whoever has this GIFT, then tries to remove the lord's gift off of the person's forehead and replace it with his mark 666!!!!!

Then I looked at all my past; all my past in my life was

wrong. At the age of 17, when I was in Iran, sleeping in the park in the darkness, I heard a voice saying, the sky is the same wherever I go. I went to the wrong uncle in Tampa, Florida. The uncle that took almost $150000 from me took 10 years of my life plus all my money. I was in the wrong marriage with the wrong family, wrong friends who interfered in my life. After my divorce, then Satan took me to the past and smoked one pack of cigarettes every day nonstop; I burnt $50000 cash with my own hands, and he made me go buy a gun to kill or hang myself with the ties inside the dark closet my son saw me in the dark closet for several months). I lost three paid-off houses, then moved to California , had that accident on the way to California, ended up in the jail for a week, went to wrong people in California. I came back and got another house; it was completely the wrong house. I brought a homeless woman into that house to help her, but she turned out to have a devil spirit in her. She stole all my stuff plus all my documents with some money, she told me it was better I follow my son to Jacksonville. I did, but I was literally in the middle of hell, sleeping in my car on the hot days and nights with Florida's mosquitos. The armies of demons had been after me every day of my life since I was born; they wanted me to stay living in the past, and they tried to keep me in confusion until I would commit suicide. I used to be a smart, prospered, and successful man with three paid-off houses. How did I end up on the street and the shelter? How can that be? I paid $210000 to my ex, and I ended up on the streets of Florida and Georgia and finally in the shelter. That is really amazing!

In every point of my life, something would bring me up, and another thing would bring me down. Look at the lord's power and majesty.

Dave told me from the beginning it is going to be a heavy task for you, as Satan will not let you go that easily, he will come after you. Are you sure you want to do this job? I stated YES! Nothing can bring me down. Then two days later I lost my job at JBS. I feel this was not a bad thing as it gave me the time I needed to write this book and get my word out about the Lord.

Peter, the prophet that I met inside the Spanish church, prospered, and he lost everything.

Dave, after doing good things, he ended up being homeless.

I have also been homeless after being so prosperous. I am sure there are more people like us. The devil can affect your life in many ways he can.

After this research, the sign of the lord is marked on your forehead. I texted Dave and asked him if this was true, that Satan was after me at every point of my life; he took everything from me, and then he tried to take away the most important piece of my life, the Lord's gift, to remove the lord's sealed mark off my forehead (Holy Spirit), he did not succeed. He said yes, all your past was controlled by the devil, but your present and your future are in lord's hands. He said, the Satan is still after you, he will try his best here and there little by little to bring you down, and he is still trying to bring you down. You will have some obstacles ahead of you, but you are protected by the lord and his angels.

He was absolutely right; I could feel it in my soul. Before I ended up in Indiana, I felt nothing, and I had no life in me; I didn't want to play music for 5 to 6 years, didn't want to eat or drink water, and didn't want to stay alive, but since I received the first lord's message when I was in Indiana, I was changed, the lord cleansed my soul, because my soul and my body were hammered by the Satan for any years almost all my past. Another miracle from God was when I got to Green Bay, Wisconsin. While I was in the hotel, right before I started working for JBS, something made me go to Facebook and create an account. Before I got to Green Bay, I had no interest in a relationship, but something drew me to Facebook. The first Woman I sent a message to and she responded in a few hours. Her name was Kitty L., there were many women who were interested in me, but she was chosen for me. She has helped me with the book and has always been there for me; she has been very supportive and respectful. Unlike the relationships, I have had in the past. Now, I love playing piano and guitar, and I love to listen to and play worship songs. These songs are repairing my broken soul. Now, I can feel and sense it; I am on the right track after nearly 50 years of my life; I am in the lord's hands. Amen.

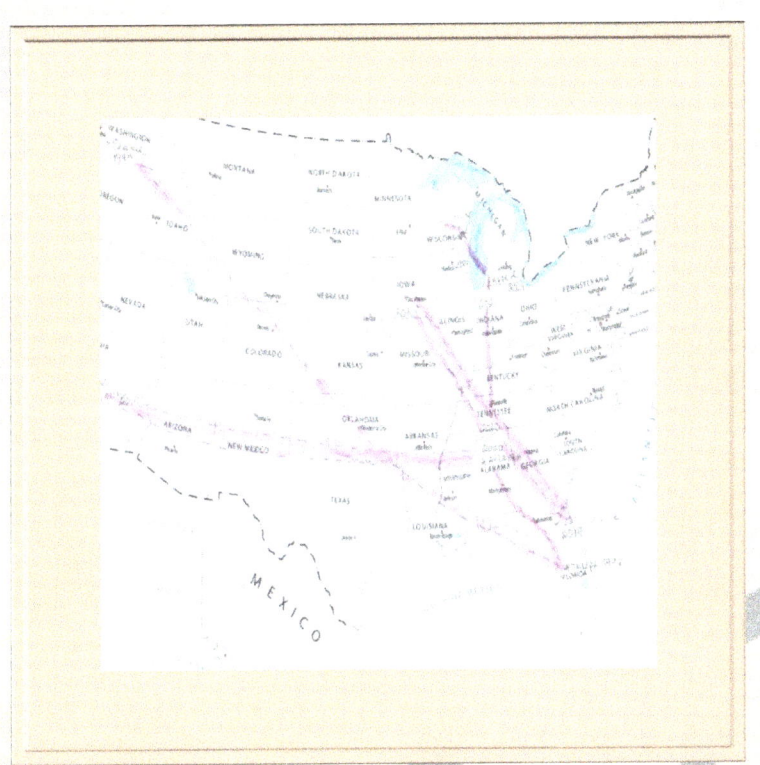

My travels in the United States and most I did without owning a car.

Chapter 2

I am not the King of this world, I am the king of Another world (John18:36)

I was blinded by the devil and the world but the lord opened my eyes.

This is my journey with you to the real creator.

Follow me and you will find the truth and I will prove it to you with all the facts.

You only need a little faith to believe that Jesus the messiah's lineage, started from Abraham, Isaac, Judah, and Jesse and all the way to David, according to the bible, the book that was, is and will stay alive.

Nobody can deny that Jesus wasn't on earth. Nobody can deny that Jesus did perform many miracles. Nobody can deny that Jesus went on the cross.

Before Jesus came on earth, the prophets in the Old Testament prophesied his coming, the exact way he would be coming, what he would do and how exactly he would be crucified and finally resurrected and return back to Father, the CREATOR OF ALL. Isaiah (9:6)

Jesus himself knew how exactly he would be crucified and, finally, how he would be resurrected to heaven and return to Father (A complete mission).

As we know, Mary and Joseph did not sleep together like any other couple to conceive Jesus. Jesus' conception was totally different than any other conception on earth. His conception was originally designed by the most powerful power of all. It had to be totally different. Do you know why? The answer is, "THE HEAVEN, THE MOST BEAUTIFUL PLACE OF ALL". I'll explain in more detail.

Heaven is a saint place, a place of mercy, a place where there's no sin, fault, or fear; there's no flesh or bones; nothing decomposes; and everything lasts forever and ever. Heaven is a completely pure place, not even close to what we even think about. We are not supposed to know what exactly is going on in heaven. It is a full secret. We will only know when we get there.

Heaven is the place of power, the highest power of all, much beyond our human mind imagination. There are no tanks, guns, warships, no weapons of any kind, and there is no oxygen. The environment is like the space. Again, this is a place of the highest power of all. It is totally different than anything on earth. It is the most beautiful place in the universe.

We humans were originally designed from there, a complete and pure place. Heavenly Father, the Creator was the architect of us and everything we see. He knows every inch of our physically and mentality human design and structure. He is also the one that created heaven. He knows all the past, present, and all the future. The Father, Jesus, Holy Spirit, Angels, and Apostle Spirit, all in heaven, can read our minds from billions of miles or kilometers away. They know what we think if we think in positive or negative ways. They are so powerful that only with one prayer, order and breath can make us a better life or wipe out the human race and everything on earth in a blink of an eye. Remember the Noah's flood. But their mercy and love for us won't let that happen; their mercy and love won't bring misery and destruction on the human race or everything on earth. They created the earth, designed it, and decided where it was supposed to be in space. They are the actual ones that designed all the life chain on earth.

It is very simple: nothing comes from nowhere. There is a saying, "Nothing is for free".

They designed the animals, they gave every creature a limited ability of functioning and thinking power, as we know every animal and bird is limited in thinking power. It is the same as when, for example, Microsoft or Apple they make some powerful computers with more or less memories and abilities.

Heaven created everything pure for what it is supposed to be in order to continue this life's chain on earth. They are not human; they are powerful, pure spirits. They own us and everything on earth, including the earth itself. What we humans invent, the first idea originally comes from them. Heavenly Father, Jesus and the Holy Spirit know all the past, present and they already know the future for the next millions years on earth. They know the human, and everything on the earth's needs. For example, they sent the information regarding how electricity should be invented to the right person at the right time, to Edison. Edison originally did not invent the electricity. The first push of information was sent from heaven to Edison's mind and spirit; then, Edison put the design on paper, and then offered it to mankind. Remember, God said, let there be light. Also, God gave electricity to mankind, all because of his love and mercy. The heavenly father created everything.

The 12 music notes were originally designed from heaven. Remember this: these music notes did not come from anywhere or by evolution. I am musician; I know the space between these 12 notes is so clear, precise, exact and complete that no human or evolution is able to create or make them. Our creator created and designed these notes for us to play, perform and worship our creator. There are worship songs that no Christian man or woman has the ability to write; these special songs come originally from heaven. Believe me; there are many more emotional and spiritual Christian songs in heaven than on earth. There are much better instruments in heaven than on earth. Again, the same thing, the instruments on earth originally were not created or invented by the musicians on earth many years ago; the design and structure of our instruments are sent from heaven to the right person at the right time, and then the person put it on paper. The 12 music notes, the songs and the instruments were originally designed from heaven for humans to play, to sing and to glorify our Creator, but we humans take these heavenly gifts to another level.

I tell you why!!! Have you ever thought why there are 12 months in a year, why we have 12 hours half day and 24 hours full day? Why do we have 12 music notes? Why did Jesus choose 12 disciples, then 12 disciples turned to 12 apostles? Why Jesus was born in the 12th month of December? Why do we have 12 days of Christmas? Why did Jesus question the religious scholars when he was 12 years old? There are 12 tribes in Israel, and 12 foundations under the wall of Israel, which hold the 12 names of the 12 apostles are marked or

61

printed on there. Why to all these questions? There are many more references about the number of 12.

The answer is because number 12 is a complete and precise number. Look at this in a very simple way: if we would have 11 or 13 month in a year, then we wouldn't have a full year; the earth would not revolve around the sun correctly. If we would have 11 hours and 59 minutes half day or 23 hours and 55 minutes, then we wouldn't have a full day again that would change the way the earth revolves around the sun. If we would have 11 or 13 music notes, then we wouldn't have the music that we have now and we would have different kinds of music or we probably wouldn't have music on earth at all.

All these are designed and structured from heaven; only the saint of all can create all these things. Again, let's be honest with ourselves: there is no way humans or evolution can create and design these things; they did not come by accident or coincidence. They are all made and created by the highest power, the same one that created the heaven, "OUR HEAVENLY FATHER," the one that created everything, the superpower of all time, the most perfect one. I know it is hard for some people to believe and understand this. But as I said before, nothing comes out of nowhere. Let me give you a couple of simple examples before I go to the main parts of the book. We all know that A country is established by somebody, A president or A king, and A State by a governor. A company is established by A boss. The President, the governor, the King or a company's president loves their country, state or company. No matter if these Main individuals do a good job for their country, state or company, they always have obstacles and disagreements with them.

The Enemy!!!!

There is always somebody, a group or people that disagree with these MAIN Big Individuals and their policies. It is all proven in human history on earth. Their enemies always try to go against these MAIN BOSSES. Then, their enemies try to create their own group to somehow get some kind of power and maybe separate themselves from the MAIN BOSSES. Remember there are always agreements and disagreements in everything, even in small or biggest families or animals (+ Positive ideas against - Negative ideas).

These two are always in a fight. This is applied anywhere in the universe, even between the stars and the planets.

This agreement and disagreement applied in heaven as well, very long ago in the HEAVEN itself.

There was a time in heaven, a very long time ago that a group of ANGELS were not in agreement with GOD, THE FATHER, THE CREATOR OF ALL. This group of angels did not agree with GOD's rules, policies and commandments. Then this group of angels regrouped and created their own god or president, "SATAN", THE DESTROYER. (JUDE 1:6 KING JAMES VERSION)

Then, GOD kicked them out of heaven. (Luke 10:18) (Matthew 25:41), But SATAN is still not done yet; Satan was and is still in disagreement with GOD, the creator of all. GOD is the one that created the heaven and the earth. The best of Satan's strategy is to go after whatever GOD created and creates his own chaos and destruction, then establish his own agenda, rules and power. Remember this: the angels are very powerful; they don't have tanks or weapons to fight but they

63

have power (Spirit) that GOD gave them. This group of angels that went against GOD and created their own god, "Satan", have almost the same powers (Spirit) but in a different manner, in a negative way with negative energy.

The Satan's targets or victims are the humans and the earth. The humans were created by GOD to have some kind of control on earth, on animals, trees and anything else on it. Also, God designed it so that the human can have some kind of peace while living on this planet. Satan, the devil and demons are dark spirits; they have power to distract, manipulate, destroy and they are the best chaos creators. When they have the human in their power, then they have their main victims against GOD himself. It is the same as when two countries start war against each other, two kings or presidents fight against each other. But the Satan's war against God is totally different than the war on earth. It is an invisible war. This war is far more dangerous than the two regular wars in earth's history. GOD's angels versus Satan's devil or demons are always fighting against each other. They are the longest enemies and have the longest warfare in the universe. Now, let me tell you what kind of powers I am talking about. (Revelations 12:7-9)

I will start with an example: let's say, someone or a family had a horrible accident or crash on the road. This accident was so severe that you cannot believe everyone in this family survived this serious accident. Then you say, this family had Angels around them; otherwise, this would be impossible for this family to have survived this severe accident. You say the angels saved this family.

An angel is able to move a mountain with only a prayer and do unthinkable things beyond human imagination. They have superpowers but much less than their creator: God (Psalms 103:20), Jesus and the Holy Spirit. The angels are authorized by GOD to do their job (Psalms 91: 11-12),

I love the angels.

There are two invisible powers: good versus evil. The angel's job is always to do good and positive things for humans, the earth and anything on it. (Daniel 10:13, Revelations 12:7-8, 20:1-3). Satan's job is to do the opposite and create negative things like destruction, manipulation and destruction, causing confusion and all kinds of evil thoughts for the human.

These two powers are the same as the war between positive pole and negative pole. These two poles are always at war. The demons and evils can be killed only by these powers: Heavenly Father, Jesus, the holy spirit, the angels and the apostles' spirits. No one else in the universe can kill them, one and only those spirits can kill and destroy them. I think I gave you enough information about THE POWER OF HEAVEN and THE POWER OF SATAN, THE TWO INVISIBLE POWERS.

Now, I like to go back to Jesus' conception and his birth. As I said before, the heaven is a place of all saint spirits; there is no flesh, bone, stomach, food, water, there are no houses, roads, factories or anything else like on earth. It is a pure saint place, and not every spirit can enter it. It is the place where Jesus's conception and miracle was sent from to Mary's womb by the Holy Spirit.(Matthew 1:18-25, Luke 1:26-38) Jesus, the son of God's conception, could have only originated from a saint place, it could not have happened on earth with humans, because humans are not saints and perfect. It is the most precious gift from God. It was all prophesied in the bible. Also, the bible is a book that was originally created from heaven; it is a book that was created for humans. This is the same way when a country or new president puts his agenda in their book for their people to follow. The Bible is a book that tells about the past, presence and the future; it is unchanged and it is the book of Saints.

As we know, Jesus questioned the Jews religious leaders when he was 12; the saintly spirit (the Holy Spirit) was and is in him, and at the same time, it was all meant to be, which was prophesied: when it would happen, in what age and where he would be crucified, resurrected and return to his father. (Matthew 23:1-12)

It was a mission that had to start and end at the right time and in the right places. Jesus never had a girlfriend, house, money, wife, land or anything else; he even never had sex. All because he came originally from saint, he was a saint and he always stays this way forever.

At the age of 30, Jesus chose 12 disciples; these disciples were special. They were not from rich families, they were already chosen even before Jesus called them. The disciples didn't understand in the beginning what was going on and why they were in front of Jesus, and then Jesus taught them many things. It was hard in the beginning for the disciples to understand Jesus's ultimate goal. Jesus talked in parables most of the time, and the disciples did not understand him or his message.

Later when Jesus performed some miracles in front of them, then the disciples gradually started to understand what was going on. Jesus already knew he would make it and he would reach his ultimate goals.

I tell you some of his precious miracles.

I start with the biggest one:

1- He rose up a dead man (Lazarus) after 4 days. (John 11:1-44) As you know, when someone dies, the very first organ in the body that stops functioning is the HEART (it doesn't matter human or animal). When the heart stops, then the blood flow stops moving throughout the arteries, veins, and vessels inside the body. Then the blood starts becoming thick everywhere, then after a few hours or five hours, the body starts decomposing; it means that this person is completely done for good; there's no way for his or her return back to life. As it is in the bible, Jesus prayed to heavenly father John 11:41-43 and he ordered for the dead to march to stand up and walk. You think why Jesus was able to do this? Because, as I said before in this chapter, our human body, inside and outside is designed by Heaven's Father. He knows every inch of our body structure.

Heavenly Father made us all. It is the same as this simple example: when Apple Company designs a smartphone. The Apple company knows everything about the design on that particular phone. If anything goes wrong with that phone or even if that phone goes completely dead, The Company can fix it and bring it back to life. Remember this: in order for Lazarus to come back to life, Jesus had to pray to heavenly father, which means in a short period of time, Lazarus's physical body had to change completely from a dead body to a life living body. This is exactly what happened. (John 11:1-44)

2- Another Jesus miracle, was when he was with his disciples inside a boat (Matthew 8:23-27, Mark 4:35-41, Luke 8:22-25). While he was sleeping, there came a very heavy storm; the disciples were scared of storm. They were afraid of drowning. They called Jesus for help, and Jesus told them if you have little faith, you can stop this storm, then Jesus prayed to the heavenly father and the storm was calmed.

3- There was a time when the disciples tried to catch fish while they were in the boat but they couldn't; then Jesus prayed and they got plenty of fish. (John 6:9)

4- In the same day, they had plenty of fishes for 5000 people but they only had a few loaf of breads and there were lots of people that had no food or places to live. The apostles told Jesus, we don't have enough bread for all these people. (Mark 6:30-44)

5- There was a woman who had been suffering from hemorrhage for twelve years, and thou she spent all she had on physicians, non-one could cure her. She came behind Jesus and touched the fringe of his clothes, and immediately her hemorrhage stopped. (Luke 8:43-48)

6- Jesus heals two blind men. (Mark 8:22-26)

Jesus did 37 different miracles. They are all online if you would like to refer them.

We need to be honest with ourselves, we need to put our

pride away and think honestly and deeply. How a man can do these things? In the earth's history, there never has been anyone that can do any of these miracles. There has to be only one person that can perform these miracles, a person that has mighty power and this person has to have a direct contact with the creator. This person should be GOD and be very, very close to GOD. As the bible says, Jesus said: JUST BELIEVE THAT I AM IN THE FATHER AND THE FATHER IS IN ME. (John 14:10-11)

Stopping a storm is not a simple task, only a person with divine power can do this. This person is the creator. This is the same as when Jesus knows every inch of our human body; he even can read our mind from the farthest distance in universe. I give you another example when Jesus could see the future (Matthew 24) (John 16:33).

Jesus also knew the past:

There was a woman that had an affair and committed adultery. Then, about 20 Jewish religious leaders brought that woman to courtyard to be stoned. They also invited Jesus to get his opinion. They asked Jesus, which one of us should throw the first stone on this woman? Then Jesus told them, "Only he who has never sinned may throw the first" (John 8:3-11)

Then, the Jewish religious leaders got quiet and had nothing to say. Then, one by one left the courtyard. Then Jesus told the woman," Go and sin no more". What do we learn from this? Jesus knew all those Jewish religious leaders; he knew their inside and outside. He knew all of their past and, of course, all their future. We are talking about a mighty power, a POWER beyond our human ability to think, even beyond our imagination.

Jesus also could see Satan, the devil and demons. He has the power to see these dark spirits. At the last super, Jesus told his disciples, the scripture will be fulfilled, one of you will betray me, I have no time, the prince of this world (SATAN) is waiting for my departure. Then the disciples asked him sir, which one of us will betray you? Then Jesus told them, he himself knows who he is Matthew 26:20-25.

As you see, Jesus could foresee the future; he had so much mercy on his betrayer that he never mentioned his name and he knew everything. He knew every moment, of what will happen to him in the next couple of days. Judah betrayed Jesus only for a little bit of money and he finally handed him to the high authorities.

The news was spreading in the region that the messiah was performing lots of miracles, and the Jewish leaders were becoming jealous. They did not like to have a competitor and were scared someone like messiah would take over their power and kingdoms. Then, they set some amount of money to anyone who would arrest the Messiah.

Peter, one of his disciples, told Jesus, I won't let you get arrested, then Jesus told him, there will come a time that you deny me three times, which was exactly what happened. (Mark 14:27-31)

Jesus, lamb of God, without any resistance or fear, he ended up in front of King Pilate. (Matthew 27:1-2, 11-26)Then Pilate asked Jesus, I heard you claim to be the king of Jews. Is this true? Then Jesus replied, "I am not the king of this world; I am

70

the king of another world". Then Pilate told the Jewish leaders, I don't see any wrongdoing from this man. Then people and the Jewish leaders said if you don't crucify this man, then you are not our friend anymore. Then Pilate told them again, I don't see any wrongdoing in this man, I hand him to you but I wash my hands from this man's blood. He handed Jesus to the leaders and the people. The soldiers spit and spat on Jesus's face. They made a crown of thorns that they placed on his head. They gave Jesus a heavy cross to carry a long distance to the mountain called SKULL, setting it up there and Jesus himself would go on top of it. He had to put his both hands on each other, then soldiers hammered a long nail into middle of his hands, then did the same to both his feet.

Can you imagine the blood that flowed from his hands and feet from where the nails were hammered into his body?

Jesus was thirsty; there was only a little wine, and someone put a little wine around his lips but the wine had vinegar in it.

There were two criminal man each beside Jesus, one of them asked Jesus, "If you are the messiah, then why don't you save yourself and us and the other said, "Jesus, remember me when you come to your kingdom," and Jesus replied, "Today you'll be with me in paradise, this a solemn PROMISE" Luke (23:39-43).

It was at noon, the darkness fell across the whole land for three hours, until 3 o'clock; the light from the sun was gone and suddenly, the thick veil hanging in the temple split apart. One of the soldiers pierced Jesus's side with a spear to make sure he was dead.

This fulfilled the scripture, "Not one of his bones shall be broken, and they shall look on him whom they pierced." (John 19:36-37)

Jesus's last prayer was, "Heavenly Father, forgive them for they don't know what they're doing; I commit my spirit to you". Then he died and his spirit resurrected from his earthly body. (Luke 23:34)

A rich man had bought a tomb for Jesus' body. Early Sunday morning while it was still dark, Mary Magdalene came to the tomb and found the stone was rolled aside from the entrance. (Luke 24:2)

Then she ran and found Peter and another disciple, told them the Lord's body was taken away from the tomb and I don't know where is taken. Peter and other disciples went to the tomb. They notice that Jesus's body had been removed; there is only a white cloth when Jesus had on.

This fulfilled the scripture, which says, "He would come back to life". 16:10 Psalms

The disciples went home; then Mary came back to the tomb crying and weeping, then she saw two white-robed angels were sitting at the head and foot of the place where the body of Jesus had been lying. Then Angles asked her, "Why are you crying?", and Mary said, because they have taken away my lord, and I don't know where they have taken him. Then she glanced over her shoulder and saw someone standing behind her, it was Jesus, but she didn't recognize him! Jesus asked her, "Why are you crying? For whom are you looking for?"

NOW, LET'S GO BACK TO THE EVENTS: Jesus had mercy on people, performed lots of miracles and did good things, but the people still didn't believe him or accept him as messiah, their savior; they had no mercy on him. A man that didn't do anything wrong, he was whipped and they spit on his face. He was hungry, thirsty, tired. He was filthy, most likely having filthy cloth on him and carrying that big cross, then after all, having two long nails on his body and finally was pierced by a spear on his side.

HONESTLY WHAT ELSE!!

A brutal way to kill a saint of all and an innocent man, but him as Lamb of God at the end, he still had mercy and love for the two criminals that were crucified next to him. Jesus told these truthful words to the two criminals." TRUELY I TELL YOU, TODAY YOU'LL BE WITH ME IN PARADISE" (Luke 23:43). Look at his authorities!!!!

This is beyond our imagination. It was only nearly 20 generations ago when Jesus was on earth. It wasn't too long ago. Now, you put yourself in Jesus's place. Would you want to go on the cross and give up your life that easy and die in that brutal manor? Do you really think Jesus could not save himself from that horrible death? Do you think a man, a saint that brought back a dead man after four days, could not save himself from that horrible event? Believe me, a man that brought back a dead man after four days could have the biggest mansion on earth, but Jesus had no house, properties, lands, wife or kids. He had nothing and because of his mercy and love, he still gave up his last things for humanity: his life and his last breath. He only had a mission to accomplish and go back home. YOU THINK WHY because he DID NOT belong to this world. He was/is originally from heaven. As I mentioned above, there are no kind of material things in heaven, and since Jesus is the closest to God, then he does not belong to this world, this world that is now dominated by Satan. JESUS WAS NOT A REAL MAN LIKE US. HE WAS A MAN WITH THE HOLY SPIRIT IN HIM!!!

As Jesus was crucified, and all those horrible events that he went through, he could see the Heavenly Father, the Holy Spirit and Angels in heaven waiting on his return. They were all in heaven watching him and waiting for his safe return. Also, at the same time, Satan, the prince of this world also, was watching and waiting for his return to heaven, because Satan couldn't stand Jesus being on earth. They were and they're still, the two longest enemies in universe.

Again, Jesus did not belong to this sinful world, because he was and is the highest saint of all. Very simple: he only had a mission to accomplish on earth and go back home. A saint spirit never fades or dies; it stays alive forever. I gave you all the tools that you need to find your true God and only creator. People, we are here on earth for a very short period of time, the earth does not belong to us, and we are only passing through. We came naked to this world and we go back naked; no matter where we go after here, we still will go naked. It doesn't matter, if we have $1 in our pocket or millions of dollars in our bank accounts; we'll still leave this world with ZERO. There had been rich or millionaires many generations before we come here on this planet and they all left with zero; right now, most of them wish they give all the money that they had and be on this earth for only 5 minutes. You have no idea where they are NOW. Right now they are in a place that you really don't want to be at all. I promise you this.

Peter, the prophet and SEER that I was within the church in Atlanta, Georgia, told me a story. He said, there was a millionaire king in one of the Middle East Arab country (I forgot which country he mentioned), and the king all of a sudden fell down and died. He did not know God. Peter said you have no idea where he is now. Then he said, right now, this king wishes to give up all the money that he had and be on this earth for only 5 minutes!!!! You think what Peter meant by saying this?

The answer is: ETERNAL HELL

Satan, the destroyer, wants you to not know your real God and savior. He wants you to stay in confusion and distract you. He wants you to go by his ideas. He wants you to go in any direction that he directs you to go to. Satan doesn't want you to know about your only creator. Satan doesn't want you to know about the eternal hell. I do not want to mention this about any religion in this book. But Satan wants you to spend millions of dollars on huge the buildings to worship and feed animal status as your gods while in your countries, there are lots of homeless, poor and sick people on your streets living in cold or hot weather. The Satan is very happy and he doesn't want you to know the truth. You are giving Satan exactly what he wants. He is invisible, but he is out there after you.

This is very simple: there are only two invisible superpowers, we don't see them but they see us, because they are spirits. SAINT SPIRITS versus DARK SPIRITS, that's all.

Christianity is not a religion; it is a true faith, very, very, powerful.

When you understand these three things, then you are on

the right track: Heavenly Father (the creator), Jesus and the Holy Spirit (Holy Ghost). The earth, the human and all the things on it belong to them, but the human is being drawn toward the Satan. Satan does everything opposite from the saints. Most of the earth, including the human, the weather, the climate, the economy and everything else are heading toward the Satan's path and direction. Everything is going in opposite ways or directions.

The earth was ruled by Satan for the past 2000 years. Jesus lived on earth for 34 years. 2000+34=2034

Now we are in 2022   2034-2022=12

We came back to number 12, A COMPLETE NUMBER. Jesus will return around 2034.

NEARLY 2000 YEARS, WE ARE VERY CLOSE

Look at this: the sun is in its middle age and it is expanding every year; it is expanding like a balloon; imagine you have a balloon; the more air you pump into the balloon, the bigger and bigger it becomes and eventually will burst.

The sun is the same way. There'll come a time that it becomes so hot and at the same time expands and becomes so big that eventually, it swallows the planets very close to it; then, as it expands more and more, then it gets closer and closer to earth. At this time, all the water in oceans, rivers and creeks on earth will evaporate, all the vegetation will disappear then the sun will get so close to the earth that it also swallows the earth and that would be the of earth. Then the sun expands so much that it finally bursts out and that would be the end of the sun, the only thing that remains is the sun's main HEAVY

CORE. This is called Super Nova.

When you are in heaven, of course, if you go to heaven), then you'll see that event when the sun bursts out; you'll see the biggest explosion ever.

But after all, you're still in a good and safe place with the lord forever because when you are with him (your true God). Then your spirit never fades and dies; your spirit will stay alive forever and forever. But the spirit of Satan, the dark spirit, will fade and die.

Now, it all depends on you, which way and direction you choose to go to, Satan's direction or THE LORD'S DIRECTION, YOUR TRUE GOD, and YOUR TRUE CREATOR.

Remember, Jesus said, I am not the king of this world; I am the king of another world. This means a lot.

Chapter 3

Conclusion

This is a very brief rundown of every important event, sign and miracle that I went through. I also connect my chapter with the Jesus/Heaven chapter.

Believe me, it is worth it. Please have a little patience to read horrible stuff that I went through and also precious stuff that you see in this long journey. This is all my gifts to the Lord, our creator and humankind. Please receive my gift to you; I promise you, you'll never regret reading this. These could be life-changing for you, your kids, family, and friends. It is all worth it!!

I am not looking for a name, fame or prosperity; I am telling these because I am responsible for telling the world. To help spread the word of God, our Father.

There is a reason why I am on this planet!!! All my past was controlled by the devil, but my present and my future is in the lord's hand. I could feel the presence of the lord within me when I got to the shelter KEYS TO HOPE in Michigan City, Indiana April 2021.

While one day, I was reading the bible in the Church/shelter; I read, "Whoever finds their life will lose it and whoever losses their life for my sake will find it." (Matthew 10:39)

"THE BIBLE IS THE PAST, PRESENCE AND FUTURE.

IT IS A LIFE BOOK THAT TALKS TO ME AND YOU."

As you read in the first chapter about my life. All of my past and all the roller coaster rides of the ups and downs that I went through were already written. All that I went through was supposed to happen for me to get to this point in my life. This is a true story that I am telling you and they are indication that the lord's return is getting closer and closer. I am sure my life story is not the only one on earth. There are lots of other individuals that went through almost the same process in their life that I went through.

I will start from the beginning. Please know I do not want to repeat myself; I just feel these are events that needed to be remembered.

1- THE DEVIL WANTED ME TO STAY IN IRAN in year 1989. WHY? As I was lying on the bench inside the dark park at the age of 17, I heard a VOICE, said: "The sky is the same wherever you go to". As I said, there was no one around me inside the dark park. I even didn't have friends at that time. Then, after nearly 40 years, I found out what and who was that voice. It was the Devil. The devil knew I wanted to leave the country, and he didn't want me to leave. The devil wanted me to stay there; this way, I never get to Holland, get baptized and become a Christian. Satan/devil didn't want me to know WHO I AM, didn't want me to know about the Lord's Sealed mark on my forehead (THE HOLY SPIRIT). Satan knew one day in my life I would write this book. He was trying to avoid this from happening.

2- In the year 1990, I managed and got to Holland, then I ended up in front of a Christian man, Stephen, in the refugee camp and got baptized after two weeks. I became a Christian but I still wasn't a strong believer; I was like a small kid crawling. Garret, a Dutch older Christian man around 73 years old, told me about his father, who was a very strong believer in Christ. Garret was at his bed when his father was dying. Garret said after his dad's last breath, he saw his father's spirit departed from his dead body; his spirit went up and disappeared.

3- In the year 1997, I moved to the United States. I went through very painful stuff that one human being should have to go through.

4- In the year 2014 friend of mine, Otto, a strong believer of Christ, came to buy a keyboard from me. Otto looked into my face and said, "Jam, the lord wants you to come to him." At that time, I didn't know what he was talking about. Because I was busy making money and not paying attention to the world around me. I didn't understand what Otto told me until too late.

5- In the year 2016 got divorced; something (negative energy/the devil) was taking me through all my past and didn't let me concentrate on the future. This thing (the devil) caused me to burn up almost $50000 cash in my own house. Who would want to burn up that much cash in his own home? This energy caused me to sell all my houses. At that time, I didn't know I was surrounded by an army of devils in my own house. Then I moved to California, and after a few months, I came back to Georgia and decided to buy a house for me and my son.

6- In the year 2018 bought the new house, but it was a

totally wrong house. I did put it back on the market for sell. While the house was on the market for sell, I brought a homeless woman with her six cats to my house to help her. She turned out to have a devil spirit in her. After I found out she had devil in her, I told her she must leave the house and she said, "YOU HAVE NO IDEA WHOM YOU'RE DEALING WITH; I KNOW EVERYTHING ABOUT YOU, I FOLLOW YOU UNTIL I BRING YOU DOWN". She cursed the ground inside my house. I lost nearly $40000 in that house after selling it. Plus she stole all my documents, some money and most of the kitchen stuff.

7- In the year 2019 my EX took my son to Jacksonville after her third failed marriage. I follow my kid to Jacksonville, Florida. While I was still living in the past and horrible stuff that happened to me, I didn't know where to go and how to start my new life in that big city where I knew no one. Sometimes, I slept in my car while it was hot and sweaty. One night, a car pulled up next to my car in a gas station; the main driver started reading his bible in his car around 10 PM. Something took me to him; I told him because of this or that I lost everything and went to my painful past; the gentleman told me he normally don't come to this part of town, but something told him to come here and give me this message. Then he said the message is "DO NOT GO TO THE PAST, I SEE THEM ALL AROUND YOU; I ASKED HIM WHO ARE THEY, THEN HE SAID, THE DEMONS "YOU LOST EVERYTHING, NOT BECAUSE OF THIS OR THAT, YOU LOST EVERYTHING BECAUSE OF YOU". This Gentleman left after 20 minutes and I never saw him again.

8- In the year April 2020 in Jacksonville, the devil woman

that turned out to have devil spirit inside her called me twice to see where I was. In April, I had $360000 in my bank account; it was at the time of Covid and when economy and the stocks went down. Someone from my Ex-wife in Jacksonville told me I buy stocks. I did what he told me: right after I bought the stock, that stock went down. I waited for it to go back up. Meanwhile, I was trying to get my CDL commercial driving license. While I was looking for what CDL school I go to, a woman from CSRT CDL School in Iowa called me. She said if I go to Iowa, she can help me to get my CDL license in three weeks. She made the arrangements for me to go to Iowa to her school. A day after that, a Christian friend called me in the morning and said, "JAM, JOSHUA IN THE BIBLE CAME INTO MY DREAM, TOLD ME TO TELL TO GIVE YOU THIS MESSAGE, STAY VERY STRONG. " I listened to him but I still didn't know what he was talking about. I left Jacksonville with two other CDL students and headed to Iowa, 23 hours of driving. I was the last person that had to drive the rental car; while I was thinking about my son Elijah, I went over the speed limit, got pulled over by the police and got a speeding ticket. When we got to Iowa CDL School, I called the recruiter; I told her I got a ticket on the way here. Then she told me because of the speeding ticket, I can't attend the school. Then I told her give a bus ticket so that I go back to Jacksonville. Finally, she sent me to the bus station; I got the ticket then we headed back to Florida. After one hour, I looked at the ticket and saw it was for Atlanta, Georgia not for Jacksonville, Florida. I was thinking what should, I do when I get to Atlanta.

9- In June 2020 got to Atlanta; I called a Christian friend of mine Otto, a Spanish man. I asked if he could help me find a place to stay somewhere. He called his pastor and got permission for me to stay at their church. When he came to pick me up, he said there was an American pastor who was a black man that stays at the church. When we got to the church the man that he was talking about was sleeping right in front of the altar. I went slept on the chairs, when I woke up in the morning, I saw the pastor walking back and forth and talking to somebody but I saw nobody around him. It was only me and him inside the church. I started to get to know this man. His name was PETER BROCKS. I asked him why you are in this church since you are an American and Peter told me he was in Guatemala in December 2019. The Lord told him, "PETER, YOU MUST GO BACK TO UNITED STATES". Then I asked Peter why you are in this Spanish church. Peter said, "THE LORD TOLD ME, PETER COME TO THIS CHURCH". Then Peter said, "HE CAME ALL THE WAY HERE TO THIS CHURCH ONLY TO CHANGE ONE INDIVIDUAL'S LIFE". I asked Peter, who is that individual? Peter pointed at me and said, "YOU". I was shocked. Then I saw Peter had a white scarf on his shoulders; my son's name was on it. ELIJAH, I asked him why you have this scarf on you with my son's name, then Peter said, "THE LORD TOLD ME PETER PUT THIS ON." It was another shock to me. I started crying; I was thinking what is going on, why me? I told Peter, I was in Jacksonville, I had a car I sold it, not sure exactly why, then on the way to Iowa got a speeding ticket, then I couldn't attend the CDL school. I could have gone to CDL School in Jacksonville to get my CDL, but I ended up in Iowa. Then I needed to go back to Jacksonville but I ended up here. Then

Peter said," IT WAS ALL SET UP FOR YOU TO GET HERE". It was another shock for me. Peter said, in 1993, he was married with a good job, house and everything, and he was very prosperous. One Sunday at his church, Jesus touched him; Peter said he knelt down on the ground and cried with tears in his eyes; he heard the most precious voice that he heard in his life. Peter said Jesus told him, "PETER, IF YOU CONTINUE THE WAY THAT YOU'RE LIVING, YOU'LL GO BACKWARD, BUT IF YOU FOLLOW ME THEN YOU'LL GO FOREWARD. Peter also told me right now, all the doors are close to me but at the right time and the right location, the doors will open. One day, he prayed for me; he said in his prayer: YOU SURRENDER YOURSELF TO JESUS, ALL YOUR SINS WILL BE FORGIVEN AND YOUR NAME WILL BE WRITTEN IN THE BOOK OF LIFE". I must emphasize that I forgot his exact prayer for me, but I remember some of it.

I saw many signs and miracles from this man. One day, I asked him, who are you? What do you want from me? Then he said, YOU HAVE NO ANY IDEA WHOM YOU'RE DEALING WITH. I AM A PROPHET AND SEER. He asked me, do you know what SEER is? I said NO and he said, "A PERSON THAT CAN SEE THE FUTURE, A PERSON THAT CAN SEE BEHIND THE THICK CONCRETE WALL. IT IS ALL BY THE POWER OF THE HOLY SPIRIT.

Peter told me, I knew you before you came here. He knew everything about me. He knew all about my past and he proved it to me. Peter could talk in my native language, Farsi; I could hear Farsi's words come out of his mouth. I asked him how you talked in my language, then he said by the power of Holy

Spirit. He kept repeating these sentences. The Lord told me, Peter, stay clean. The lord authorized me (Peter). Faith is a risk, R I S K. I was very important to Peter, I still wasn't sure why!!! He most of the time was talking in a parable like Jesus; his life was Jesus. Peter knew the whole bible; he had a thick bible. When I would ask him a question, he would say the same words and sentences in the bible. He also said he had a dream Russia would attack the US.

I ended up being with Peter in that church for about 4 months. I saw many signs and miracles from him, which I explained in the first chapter. One evening around 9 P.m., while It was only me and Peter in the church, I was lying on the seats, and Peter went in front of the altar, raised up his hands strongly, and prayed, "HEAVENLY FATHER, MY MISSION IS DONE, I AM COMING BACK HOME". Then he came toward me and said he would be leaving the church and the people of this church would never see him again. The last time I talked to Peter, I was in the hospital; he called me and said while he was in South Carolina in the hotel room after his work, Jesus touched him. Peter said he heard the same precious voice that he heard before. He said Jesus assigned him the land of Mexico, Guatemala and a couple of other South American countries. Peter also said the lord promised him that he would become US president at the right time. All the CEO's will stand in front of him and he already has the answers for all of them. I asked him how. Then he said," BY THE POWER OF HOLY SPIRIT." It was the last time that I talked to Peter. Peter got to that church and waited on me for four to five months. He knew I would get there one day. I was his mission at that that period of time. Peter, I love you.

10- In March 2021, in Atlanta, Georgia, while I was in the hospital, I met a man. After talking to him, he said he would help me to get back on my feet and he will help me with CDL. He said, but I must travel with him to Indiana stay at his girlfriend's house. He took me from Georgia to La Port, Indiana. When I was in La Port, Indiana, something was pushing me to go to the DMV driving license to get my CDL. I walked long distances to the DMV for 5 days in a row until I got all my endorsements. Police took me out of that house because it was the wrong place for me to stay there. Then I ended up in a place called "KEYS TO HOPE "; it was a shelter, a church in Michigan City, Indiana. After a week, the shelter helped me to get my CDL in four weeks but I had to attend a school in another city, La Port, Indiana. I could see the doors are gradually opening for me.

In the first day of school, there were only 6 students; I saw a woman watching me continuously; I wasn't sure why!!! Then the woman, at the break time, gradually got closer and closer to me. She introduced herself to me and said her name is Ernestine. She is a prophet; she was sent to give me the lord's message. It was another shock to my soul. She didn't give me the message right away. I could feel there was a connection between me and this woman that I met for the first time in my life. I could see I am important to this woman. Ernestine took me back to KEYS TO HOPE in Michigan City with her car and left. It was around 8 or 9 PM, and while I was at the church shelter, I received a text message from Ernestine. I did read it:" I AM PREPARING YOU, SAYS THE LORD. YOU FEEL LIKE WHY ME OR HOW AM I GOING TO MAKE IT THROUGH? I CAN'T TAKE ONE MORE THING

(DISAPPOINTMENT). GOD SAYS IT IS NOT ON YOU BUT TO TRUST HIM. WHEN YOU ARE WEAK, THAT'S WHEN I SHOW UP STRONG. TRUST IN ME! YOU DON'T FEEL EQUPIMPED, BUT I AM EVERYTHING YOU NEED. I AM NOT LIKE MAN; I WILL NEVER LEAVE YOU OR FORESAKE YOU. IN THIS SEASON, GET INTO YOUR WORD AND LET IT CARRY YOU. GOD IS SAYING THAT YOU NEED TO FOCUS SOLELY ON HIM. THE ENEMY WANTS TO DISTRACT YOU BUT THE BATTLE IS ALREADY WON. YOU ARE IN A FIXED FIGHT."

After receiving this text message, I texted Ernestine, the lady that I met in the CDL school on the first day, I said thank you for the message. Ernestine texted me back and said, she didn't send me this message. Her friend of hers, who is a prophet and she is right now at the hospital in pain, SENT THIS MESSAGE TO ME. Please remember, it was only first day that I met Ernestine at the CDL school, and I even never met the other prophet lady friend of Ernestine, who that sent this message to me and was at the hospital in pain.

After 4 weeks of going to the CDL School, I finally got my CDL. Then I searched which trucking company should I go with. I went to the shelter's manager, Erica, and asked her to lady to help me to make the right decision because most of her family truck drivers. Then Erica told me, Jam, you should go with JBS trucking carrier, it is the biggest meat company in the world. Something inside me told me to listen to her, which I did. I called JBS recruiter and the recruiter, Jeff, said we want you. He did all the preparations, drug screen tests and orientation and finally got me the plane ticket to go to Green

Bay, Wisconsin. I also have to mention that sometimes, I was preaching the gospel while I was in the shelter.

In July 2021 flew to Green Bay, Wisconsin. The company got me a hotel for a few days. When I was at the hotel, I went on Facebook to look for a single woman. I had not been interested in a relationship before this, but something made me do it. I sent the first message to a lady in Wisconsin, and she replied to me about a couple of hours after that. She was very interested in me, and I was in her as well. We started chatting and finally had a few phone calls; her name was Kitty. She has been a great support to me and she edited this book for me. I told Dave later on that I had several women on the Facebook site that were interested in me. Dave said you should go with the first woman as she was chosen for you. That was Kitty.

After a few days, I started training with the company, which took 6 weeks. I finished the training, but I still wasn't comfortable with the computer inside the truck. While I was in Ohio, parked at the service center parking lot, I found out I had six DOT violations in the computer; then my boss called me and said, Jam, you can't move truck even one inch. He said we bring you back to Green Bay with another driver for a few more days of training. I got back to the Green Bay terminal and went to see the boss. After we talked and he told me what I needed to do, I left his room. All of the reason I went sat down on a chair inside the main office next to the main door. While I was sitting on the chair, I saw an older gentleman who was watching me continuously; I wasn't sure why!!!

All of a sudden, I asked the gentleman, Do you believe in Jesus? He said of course. Then I told him about my experiences with Peter for about 20 minutes, and then he came closer to me and said, "You are a soft-spoken man." Then my boss came out of his room and said, Jam, you go with Dave for a few more days of training. Dave is the 71-year-old gentleman that I was just talking to. I could see like there was a connection between me and Dave, the trainer. I went with Dave for a few days of training. We went to the first customer; it was in the evening. While we were waiting to unload, Dave said Jam, can I show you something? I said sure. He took off his shoes and socks. All of a sudden, I saw two nail crucifixion marks on his both feet, exactly where Jesus was nailed on the cross. Dave said, if I show these marks to people, the people won't believe him. I told Dave, I believe you. Dave also said he had a daughter that died from cancer and they had a very close relationship. Dave said he also had cancer some years ago; while he was on the surgery bed, he was dead. He said he died for 6 minutes and his spirit left his body; while his spirit was going farther and farther away from his body, he saw his daughter's spirit in heaven. They waved at each other until they got closer and they hugged each other, right after this a strong voice inside the light called and told him "THIS IS NOT YOUR TIME, YOU MUST GO BACK, YOU HAVE A MISSION TO ACCOMPLISH". Then Dave's spirit came back to his body.

Then, on the last day of training, Dave had to drop me off of my truck at the Ohio service center. It was about 45 minutes left to get to my truck; while Dave was driving and I was on the passenger seat, Dave turned his face and started talking. I saw another person in his face, a very serious person inside his face; I was scared. It wasn't Dave's face; it was someone else.

While I was watching him said, "Jam, ME AND THE ANGELS WERE AROUND YOU FOR QUITE SOMETIMES FOR YOUR PROTECTION; YOU WILL MEET THE LORD. THE LORD LOVES YOU. YOU WILL BECOME ONE OF US. YOU GOT THE LORD'S GIFT; THE LORD GOT YOU THIS JOB THIS WAY YOU WORK, AND ALSO, YOU HAVE ENOUGH TIME TO SPEND TIME WITH HIM. YOU MUST HAVE LOTS OF RESPECT FOR THE LORD WHEN YOU MEET HIM. THE LORD HAS PLAN FOR YOU. CONTINUE PREACHING, BUT IF SOMEONE DOESN'T WANT TO LISTEN TO YOU, JUST LEAVE HIM BEHIND. While I was watching and listening to him I started crying and tears running from my eyes. Then, Dave said, let's pray. I prayed with him. He left me at my truck and went on his way.

There were two things I didn't ask him:

1. How long he and the angels were around me

2. What was the lord's gift that I Have?

Next day, Dave called me and said Jam, did you see another person inside his face while he was talking to me yesterday. I told him YES; I saw another serious person inside your face. He said it was one of the apostle's spirits that enter into his body and communicates. Then Dave told me, please read the Ephesians book in the New Testament in the bible. I said, ok, I do. Dave also said I was his mission.

Then I did read the Ephesians first time but I still didn't understand why Dave wanted me to read the Ephesians book!! I was thinking before I call him and tell him I did read the book, I need to read it again. After I read the first chapter, I read where Paul says, "WE ARE MARKED AS BELONGINGS TO CHRIST BY THE HOLY SPIRIT, and WHO LONG AGO HAD BEEN PROMISED TO ALL OF US CHRISTIANS. HIS PRESENCE WITHIN US IS GOD'S GUARANTEE THAT HE REALLY WILL GIVE US ALL THAT HE PROMISED. AND THE SPIRIT 'S SEAL UPON US MEANS THAT GOD HAS ALREADY GRANTED US THAT GUARANTEE TO BRING US TO HIMSELF. THIS IS JUST ONE MORE REASON FOR US TO PRAISE OUR GLORIOUS GOD."

We were marked as belonging to Christ by the Holy Spirit!!

This got my very attention. I went online and researched more about it, and I found amazing stuff. "THE LORD'S GIFT SEALED MARK ON OUR FOREHEAD" (THE HOLY SPIRIT). Then I read more and researched more, and found out this is what the Satan is after. It is what Satan tries to find and destroy the person's life, whoever has this GIFT, then tries to remove the lord's gift off of the person's forehead and replace it with his mark 666!!!!!

Somewhere, I also read online when you find out you have the lord's sealed mark on your forehead (the Holy Spirit), then this indicates the LORD'S RETURN is getting closer. When you know you have this gift, then you are responsible for bringing others to Christ.

After reading all this, then you will understand this is why, for so many years I could feel a negative energy was after me and bothering me for so long in my life.

❖ The devil woman that I brought inside my house said, I know everything about you. I follow you until I bring you down.

❖ That's why the person at the gas station said, I see them all around you; you lost everything because of you.

❖ That is why Peter the prophet came all the way from Guatemala to that church and was waiting on me for four months until I got there and change my life. He said he came all the way to that church only to change one individual's life. I asked him who that was, and he pointed at me and said, "YOU".

❖ Then I ended up in Indiana in the CDL School in front of Ernestine, the prophet that sent me the lord's message. Remember, it was the first time that I met this woman in my life.

❖ Then I ended up in Wisconsin at the right time and right place in front of Dave.

❖ Dave said all my past was controlled by the devil, but now my present and my future are in the lord's hand.

"DAVE ALSO SAID I WAS HIS MISSION"

As I looked into all my past, I see many up and downs I had, I went through horrible stuff that very few human beings would go through.

Chapter 4

HEAVEN

Nobody can deny, he or she doesn't remember their past. You remember when you were a small kid, grew up, became a teenager, and turned into an adult. Then you say, oh wow, the time and those years passed by very quickly. You remember the ups and downs that you had in all your past and present. You can't deceive yourself. You know your life will end one day, but not sure when!!! You know you won't be on this planet very long; this is exactly what you see every year: winter, spring, summer and fall come and go. The planet earth circles around the sun's orbit once a year; everything and every life chain goes forward, and nothing will go backward. This life's chain includes your life and my life; while we go forward then one day, our life will end. We are all limited. But there is one question that everyone asks himself or herself: what was the reason I came on this planet and where will I go after here when I am gone? If you believe that you have a soul, ask yourself, your body will decay but what will happen to your soul? As you know our soul is an energy that was given to us before when we were conceived in our mother's womb. This soul and energy stays with us after when we come out of our mother's womb and all the way till we die. Do you ever ask yourself where your soul came from? The answer is your soul did not come by the evolution. Evolution cannot create or design. The energy inside your soul was designed by a SUPERPOWER. This superpower had a purpose to give you this energy. This superpower knew you before they gave you your soul/energy. This superpower is not a MAN. His power and abilities are way beyond our imagination. This superpower is invisible. He can see you through your life, but you don't see him; this is where your faith comes in. Remember this: a human cannot design and shape another human. Again, the superpower that designed me and you cannot be a human. Whatever you and I see on this planet was originally designed by him. We are all designed on this planet for a very short period of time. Your physical and earthly body will decay, erode and fade away, but you also have a soul/energy that has been with your earthly body throughout all your life. The question is: where does your soul/energy go?

The same superpower that gave you your soul/energy when you were in your mother's womb decides where your soul will go!!! As I mentioned before in Jesus/heaven chapter, most human beings, including many generations before us, our generations after us, waste his or her time by knowing many different (Gods). Many Gods cannot design and create man; if so then there would be fights between these gods in some way or another. The same as if a country would have two or more presidents. Sooner or later, there will be fights and disagreements between these COUNTRY PRESIDENTS and finally, the country will go in the wrong direction. This is the same as, if you and I would have several different designers and creatures (Gods)!!!

A God is a Spirit, a God that has superpowers way beyond what you and I think. Believe me, what you and I see on this planet is nothing compared to the abilities and power that God has. Our God is very patient and smart. His mercy and love is way beyond our understanding. He is a God that can give life and take life with the blink of an eye. There is only one person that in this universe that showed the power of true God, Jesus, the messiah!!!

This is very important: JESUS, THE MESSIAH, WAS THE ONLY PERSON THAT HAS THE POWER OF TRUE GOD AND NO ONE ELSE ON EARTH'S HISTORY HAD THE POWER TO SHOW THE POWER OF OUR TRUE GOD.

Jesus, did perform all the miracles and signs through his father in heaven. Jesus said, "You know the true God only through me." He also said, "He is the only one that can take you and show you your true God."

My message to all of you is that you are really wasting your time by trying to know your created gods. There is only and only one God; he is able to in creditable things.

Let's go back to the question: where does your soul will go when you die? I hope after reading my book and seeing how the devil can influence your life that you will start thinking about your own life and where you want to go after this life.

God is waiting. Amen

Thank you very much for reading my book. God bless you and your family.

Please check out the website often to see updates on the shelters that we have helped.

I also have plans to add short stories to the blog page.

Please check out the music page; there are some songs that I wrote that were inspired by my soul that was touched by

Jesus.

God Bless you all and your journey to God the Father Almighty! Amen

I will pray for each and every one of your souls.

Thank you

Jamshid Morrvaridy

Please check my Website often new blogs and stories to follow:

JamshidMorrvaridy.com